The
WOMAN
in the
PULPIT

The
WOMAN
in the
PULPIT

Carol M. Norén

ABINGDON PRESS/*Nashville*

THE WOMAN IN THE PULPIT

This book is printed on recycled, acid-free paper.

Library of Congress Cataloging-in-Publication Data

Norén, Carol Marie.
    The woman in the pulpit/Carol M. Norén.
    p. cm.
    Includes bibliographical references.
    ISBN 0-687-45893-5 (pbk.)
    1. Women clergy. I. Title.
BV676.N67   1992
253'.082—dc20   91-30132
                                     CIP

MANUFACTURED IN THE UNITED STATES OF AMERICA

To my parents,

Adelle Marie and Gustav Albert Norén

CONTENTS

INTRODUCTION

*T*he Sunday morning service is different when a woman preaches. Church members know this instinctively. Women clergy know it, too, though past encounters with prejudice may make them reluctant to acknowledge and work with the differences. We live in a curious era of church history, when talking about the distinctive gifts and liabilities that women bring to pulpit ministry can mean risking accusation of sexism on the one hand or strident feminism on the other. And yet, both clergy and laity can benefit from an examination of what happens when the voice proclaiming the Word is feminine.

For example, on the Sunday after Christmas, I preached on Luke 2:22-40 to a university congregation. The focus of the sermon was Simeon and Anna's response to the experience of Immanuel. Of all the comments made by worshipers after the service, two have stayed with me. A man asked why I didn't smile more during the sermon. A woman thanked me enthusiastically for my message, adding, "I never realized that Anna had a story to tell. Wait till I tell my granddaughter!—her name is Anna, too."

Although my agenda in the sermon was neither feminist nor anti-feminist, these responses from listeners reflected gender-related issues. The grandmother evidently heard a message of hope and possibility: a liberating word for herself and her granddaughter. The fact that the medium was a woman preacher's voice reinforced her perception. The man, however, experienced a level

9

of dissatisfaction that I suspect was related to our culture's expectations of women. After all, most men preachers are not noted for how much they smile in the pulpit!

What is the benefit of taking a second look at what was happening during the worship service and the conversation afterward? It is not necessarily resolving to smile more and to always include a positive role model for women in the sermon, but being able to make better-informed decisions the next time I preach. Rather than merely being frustrated by cultural filters through which people listen to a woman preacher, I can begin to anticipate those filters, and choose to work with them, work around them, or challenge them head on.

As mentioned earlier, lay people also stand to gain from thoughtful consideration of what is "different" about hearing a woman preacher. It may lead to discernment between reasonable and unreasonable expectations, or clarification of their theology of ministry and the church. It may make them more aware of sexism as it is manifested elsewhere in our society. For still others, it may enable them to claim their own integrity and ministry.

More women are enrolling in seminaries and divinity schools than ever before. In 1972, women constituted 10 percent of the student body in Protestant seminaries in the United States. In 1986, they made up 26 percent of the enrollment. In spite of the increase, a majority of these women will be the first female pastors their congregations have had—and this will make a difference to them and the churches. How will they understand and work with this difference?

Recent years have seen a proliferation of literature on issues pertaining to women and the church, particularly questions of ordination and ministry. Although some of these publications provide useful insights concerning a woman preacher's orientation to this aspect of her ministry, most of those that discuss preaching share a significant limitation: the communication event that takes place when one person addresses others in the context of worship cannot be captured in the printed word.

In his article, "Preaching as Confluence," Conrad Massa of Princeton Theological Seminary presents the thesis that preaching is comprised of four distinct components: the preacher, the listeners, what is actually said, and the context in which it occurs.[1]

Printed sermon manuscripts only reproduce one of the four: what is said. Even this is subject to misunderstanding since the inflection, pace, and gestures with which it is uttered are inaccessible to the reader. Preaching and ministry are highly interactive endeavors, reflecting relationships subject to constant renegotiation. Massa's other three elements of preacher, listeners, and context, when noted at all, are mediated through an interpreter whose editorial and theological biases may not be known. This limitation is inevitable, given that all readers do not have access to all women preachers.

There is a second limitation to the usefulness of the aforementioned types of publication for the woman hoping to grow in effectiveness as a preacher, or for others seeking insight on issues pertaining to the average woman preacher serving a local church. Persons whose sermons are published regularly are likely to be those known and respected by the editor or publisher. They have achieved a degree of fame that makes their work marketable in printed form. Therefore, limiting a study of women in the pulpit to a sample of published sermons is not likely to be representative of what all or "typical" preachers of that time or culture are doing, but rather will be representative of what preachers known by a given editor or denominational hierarchy are doing.

In this book I attempt to write *about* women preachers, acknowledging that I can speak on behalf of only one: myself. My goal is to equip women students and clergy for intentional, effective, and faithful communication of the gospel. Rather than merely presenting sermons and liturgies by women, the chapters that follow describe how they are likely to work or not work in a local church context, and the reasons for this. My purpose is not to present a lone paradigm for women's preaching, but to make women sensitive to underlying issues in their own theology and communication. A secondary goal is to enhance homiletics classes' and churches' awareness of their gender-related expectations of preachers, so that what has operated often unconsciously can be examined, and in some cases, discarded as invalid.

Because of my conviction that actual preaching events yield data that sermon events cannot, a substantial percentage of the material used in this book was gleaned from listening to women of various denominations preach in local churches across the country. Other examples were gleaned from women students in classes I have taught at Duke University Divinity School, The Iliff School of Theology (both United Methodist schools), and Princeton Theological Seminary (Presbyterian). Material from published sermons and "the electronic church" is also used, both to give the book greater scope and to include works to which nearly any reader has access.

The opening chapters of the book deal primarily with questions concerning the identity of women as preachers. The first chapter discusses the call to preach: how women experience it, respond to it, and find it affirmed or denied by their churches. My focus here is calling rather than ordination per se. There are several reasons for this: first, there is a lineage of preaching women in church history for whom ordination was not an issue. Second, there are women today who live out their call to preach in churches that do not consider women ordainable. Third, the focus of the book is on one particular aspect of ministry—preaching as it normally occurs in the Sunday worship service. It is not a systematic exploration of the meaning of holy orders. Arguments for and against the ordination of women are dealt with in depth by other authors.

Role models are the subject of the second chapter: who chooses them, what aspects of their life and work are extolled, and what positive functions may they serve for the woman in the pulpit. When an absence of role models is perceived, what impact does this have on a woman's ministry? The third chapter is closely related to this: the relationship of preaching to women's pastoral ministry. It examines what may happen when the preacher and congregation have conflicting or incongruous role models. It includes discussion of a woman preacher's understanding of authority, accountability, and professional credibility.

The fourth chapter, on self-disclosure in preaching, explores the discrepancy or fidelity between what the woman preacher believes about herself and what she proclaims in her sermons. Case studies about women preachers' self-image are presented, and examples are offered of the ways stereotypes are reinforced or challenged.

Following the fourth chapter, the discussion shifts from the woman preacher's identity to a more focused examination of the work of proclamation. The fifth chapter deals with the question of theology and interpretation. Excerpts from women's sermons are used as examples demonstrating feminist, liberation, and other hermeneutics. This is closely related to the sixth chapter, on theology in metaphor and grammar. Barbara Bate, Catherine Ziel, and other scholars suggest that women use the English language differently from men, and are therefore heard differently as well. The conscious cultivation of new theological language by some preachers is presented and analyzed.

The seventh and final chapter explores the relationship between women's preaching and its liturgical framework. In most churches, the preacher has major responsibility for deciding what else happens in the worship service, and how it occurs. Sometimes the preacher automatically follows the worship pattern established by a predecessor, but when a deliberate change is made, the preacher usually has a principle or result in mind. Examples of both "patterns" and "changes" are identified in women's leadership of worship. Sample works from the feminist liturgical movement are presented and evaluated.

I am indebted to the colleagues and friends who helped in the development of material for this book: Raymond M. Krutz and the late Norman C. Miller, who helped me to claim my call to preach; Signe and Nils John Anderson, whose support and encouragement have sustained my ministry from the beginning; Paul Rademacher, whose advice aided me in focusing on the particular possibilities and problems of women in ministry. I am grateful to Ann I. Hoch, Robert L. Wilson, and Teresa M. Berger of Duke Divinity School for reading through various drafts of this material. My deep thanks to women in my preaching class and the local church, who graciously answered survey questions, engaged in endless discussions, and allowed their work to be used as examples throughout this study. Finally, appreciation is also due Wanda D. Dunn for typing the manuscript.

Carol M. Norén
The Divinity School
Duke University

*T*he majority [of contemporary women] did not make reference to personal theophanies or cataclysmic events in describing their call.
—Carol M. Norén

*I*t was my personal desire to explain why I followed Jesus Christ to my [Jewish] friends and myself that drew me into the youth program at a nearby congregational church. I needed to defend my Christian witness and, at the same time, I wanted to take other religions seriously. My search led me to seminary and ordained ministry.
Barbara Brown Zikmund
—Twentieth-century preacher

*T*he nineteenth-century woman preacher vindicated her ministry by pointing to evidence of the Holy Spirit's anointing, biblical precedent, the number of souls converted, and other empirical signs that her work was "bearing fruit."
—Carol M. Norén

*A*nd now, my dear sister, do not be startled, when I tell you that you have been ordained for a great work. Not by the imposition of mortal hands, or a call from man, no, Christ, the great Head of the church, hath chosen you, and "ordained you, that ye should go and bring forth fruit."
—Phoebe Palmer
Nineteenth-century preacher

*O*NE

THE CALL TO PREACH

*E*ver since the apostles prayed and cast lots to find a replacement for Judas, the church has wrestled with the question of the call to ministry and how it is recognized, affirmed, or denied. Past generations did not ordinarily grant a hearing to women who aspired to become official leaders in the community of faith. Maleness was not the only requirement for ordination, but it was an unvarying one. Women who claimed a vocation had few options; they could exercise their ministry outside the church, operate within the limited spheres open to them (such as the convent), or ignore what they believed was a divine mandate.

Times have changed, along with church polity, but the idea of calling continues to be a gender-related controversy today. Although the number of women clergy in the United States increased by 98 percent between 1977 and 1986, some denominations still battle over whether or not women can be ordained.[1] When contemporary Christian women claim a vocation, some are told they must be mistaken (because they are female) while others find strong advocacy (because they are female).

The belief that she is called by God is a powerful motivating factor for the individual woman preacher or seminary student. This can be demonstrated by both personal testimonies and by more formal data-gathering. For example, the Association of Theological Schools conducted a survey of seminary students in 1988, in order to get a profile of the typical person preparing for ministry. Among other things, they discovered that significantly more women than men stated their primary reason for being in seminary was the belief that they had a call from God.[2] The percentage was highest among Roman Catholic women, although they cannot be ordained to the ministry of word and sacrament.

This chapter explores the question of vocation from several perspectives. The testimonies of contemporary women about their call to preach and/or pursue ordination are presented, and then compared with testimonies of the nineteenth- and early twentieth-century women. The similarities and differences are used to point out relationships between call and cultural/temporal context, and indicate underlying theological issues for the woman preacher and the church as a whole.

THE TESTIMONY OF CONTEMPORARY PREACHING WOMEN

Several years ago I began interviewing Protestant women seminarians and pastors, in hopes of gaining a fuller understanding of their self-image and of becoming better equipped to train them to preach. Among other issues, I wondered if women who perceived a degree of resistance to their presence in the pulpit would have a "ready defense" for the pursuit of their calling. Having begun my own theological education during the Vietnam conflict, I had met male students motivated to enroll in Master of Divinity programs by the desire for clergy deferment; for them, seminary was a place to live out their convictions concerning the war, but not a response to a call to ministry. Given the very different controversy over women's roles in the church, I was curious to learn what led them to begin the process toward ordination. I asked them whether they believed their call was to a specific aspect of ministry, and what factors had convinced them the call was genuine. I also invited them to identify people who influenced their decision.

Most of the women interviewed were comfortable with the vocabulary of "call," and described their own sense of vocation as growing gradually. One Baptist woman responded, "It was a process. At age 20 I felt called to parish work." Another Baptist said, "As a child I felt called to the ministry in general. No voice, no lightning—it just seemed to happen." An Episcopal priest interviewed said, "I went to seminary to study theology and philosophy. During field education, I gained a sense that this was what I wanted to be." Two women spoke of ordination when describing their call; one, a United Methodist, commented, "I felt called to preach at age 10 or 12, but didn't think about it much until college. I thought about entering the convent before I knew women could be ordained." The most explicit reference to divine-human interaction came from a Presbyterian woman who said, "I felt called to preach, because I like writing. I considered social work, but attending an ordination service convinced me ordination was for me. It was as though I heard a voice saying, 'as you have seen, so be it unto you.' "[3]

These women preachers did not report much in the way of resistance or impediments to their ministry. When an older, Cuban-American woman talked to me about her difficult road to ordination in The United Methodist Church, she communicated a stronger sense of her call both as a specific event and as a divine imperative than the previous subjects. God gave her a signal, she said, and overcame her objections that she was too old, battling a life-threatening illness, and apt to be rejected in a Spanish-speaking community. She didn't decide to become a minister; God decided for her, and she thanked God and said, "use me."[4]

Just as interviews supplement or illuminate the data yielded by statistical studies, so also published biographies and autobiographies provide information from women preachers about their calls to ministry. Most of the seven Episcopal women interviewed in *Women of the Word: Contemporary Sermons by Women Clergy* began seminary education for personal reasons rather than in pursuit of ordination. Only one of the seven women spoke of the decision for seminary in vocational terms: "I wanted to be a missionary as a child, no role models for preacher, very active in church; began thinking of the ministry when a suburban housewife with young children."[5]

The sermon anthology *And Blessed Is She* includes works by fifteen contemporary women of various denominations. Reflection by the preacher, usually autobiographical, follows each sermon. Of the fifteen, four discuss their call, but usually in terms of process rather than event. For example, Barbara Brown Zikmund wrote:

> . . . it was my personal desire to explain why I followed Jesus Christ to my [Jewish] friends and myself that drew me into the youth program at a nearby congregational church. I needed to defend my Christian witness and, at the same time, I wanted to take other religions seriously. My search led me to seminary and ordained ministry.[6]

Two women described specific events surrounding their call more than the call itself. Bishop Leontine Kelly did not give an account of her call here, but described the event in another essay, on preaching in the black tradition: "I taught a course on 'The Inner Life' at the Virginia Conference School of Christian Mission and there felt and responded to my own personal call to the ministry of Jesus Christ. For me the journey toward ordination was a pinnacle experience."[7]

Judith Weidman's *Women Ministers,* a collection of first-person essays by clergywomen working in the parish, reveals the same percentage of women describing their call as important to their self-understanding.

One of the best-known clergywomen in our time is Isabel Carter Heyward, whose book, *A Priest Forever,* documents events leading to her ordination to the Episcopal priesthood in 1974. She uses the term "call" in two senses: the mandate to "tell our stories, and in telling our stories manifest a new reality," and also to describe the events and process that convinced her that she was called to ordained ministry.[8] For her, the call was gradual and cumulative, a verdict reached after considering much evidence, and ultimately vindicating what she intuited from early childhood.

In *When the Minister Is a Woman,* Elsie Gibson recounted a call that seems both specific and gradual. It began with a numinous experience in her mid-teens; she described praying alone one night, and becoming aware of a stillness that deepened into total silence. Into that silence came a penetrating, questioning impression that her mind groped for words to retain. It took years of maturing and study to discern what sort of divine-human interaction it was.[9] Furthermore, Gibson did not clearly link it with her vocation as a minister in the United Church of Christ. In her chapter on "A Sense of Mission," Gibson gave examples of women who were "called" by their sense of the needs of the church or the world, through their own suffering, and through dramatic religious experiences. In reading their respective books, it becomes clear that for Gibson, a woman's call is always to work "within the system," where for Heyward, a call may challenge and/or change the institution in which that call is lived out.

What can we make of these testimonies? A careful reading discloses recurrent themes and images in the stories told by these contemporary women in ministry. First, most of the women who spoke about their call described a process rather than a specific event. A second recurrent theme in the discussion of call is uncertainty about the way it would be lived out. A third common trend in these testimonies is the emphasis on relationships in ministry. The *tasks* of ministry are mentioned less than how the preacher understands herself and others. It led me to wonder if this is a gender-related difference, since some men are ostensibly drawn to the church as an arena for exercising leadership and living out God's word through organizing and administrating.

The vocabulary used to talk about calling may also be worth further consideration. The majority did not make reference to personal theophanies or cataclysmic events in describing their call. Most of these women, who were ordained or seeking ordination, were from mainline denominations or a state church, i.e., not from groups we would call sects. Their religious communities are not countercultural. It may be that in a society where the hyperactive, Bible-quoting television preacher is fodder for late-night comedians and supermarket tabloids, the women instinctively avoided the language favored by traditions placing a high premium on personal religious experiences. It may also be that since these churches already ordained women when the data were gathered, the women legitimized their vocation using the terminology and rationale more likely to be understood and received favorably: their gifts for ministry, work record, and/or the reasonableness of the church ratifying their call.

However one accounts for the ways contemporary women articulate their call to ministry, there is unquestionably a contrast between their testimonies and those of nineteenth- and early twentieth-century North American women who believed that they were called to preach. A brief description of the religious and cultural milieu in which these women lived will help set their calls in context.

THE TESTIMONY OF PREACHING WOMEN
OF THE LAST CENTURY

Women had preached—and believed themselves called—before this time, but the nineteenth century saw a remarkable increase in the number of women participating in worship as itinerant and local preachers, exhorters, and leaders of prayer. In addition, it was during the nineteenth century that women began to make a connection between "call" and ordination in American churches; denominations were forced to deal with the issue of women's ministry in a more explicit, systematic way. Nancy Hardesty credits Charles Grandison Finney not only with championing the rights of women to preach and teach, and playing a part in the 1853 ordination of Antoinette Brown, but also articulating an understanding of ministry itself that reflected a major trend of the time and left an indelible mark on religion in America:

> Finney believed the chief end of ministry was the salvation of the soul. . . . This definition of ministry—divorced from intellectual leadership, social authority, sacramental power, and moral discipline—opened the door to women, who were being culturally defined anyway as keepers of religious values.[10]

In writing about women in evangelical, holiness, and Pentecostal traditions, Letha Dawson Scanzoni and Susan Setta suggest a number of factors that lead to a receptivity to women's calls to preach in holiness groups: an experiential theology, focused on conversion and sanctification; emphasis on the work of the Spirit; a subjective interpretation of Scripture in line with experiences; a reformist or revolutionary outlook; and a tendency to form sects with organizational ability.[11]

Two additional factors that could be found among many Protestant groups of the time were: (1) the separation of preaching from sacraments, and (2) prejudice against Roman Catholicism. There was a reciprocal relationship between the two; the Mass had the Eucharist as the center of worship, and only a priest could officiate. In Protestant frontier religion, the service might be led by a licensed preacher, an exhorter, an ordained minister, or a pious layperson, but in the days of the circuit riders, opportunities to receive the Eucharist were infrequent. The itinerant preacher who rode into a territory was judged more by a convincing testimony and the results of his or her preaching than by examination of the credentials carried in the saddlebag.

Women who believed themselves called to preach did not, then, *necessarily* perceive this as a call to ordination. They lived in a culture where many men who preached were only licensed, or had no denominational affiliation. When ordination per se was sought by women with a call, sometimes it was to have credentials within a connectional church, or to facilitate overcoming cultural prejudice against them serving in their homeland. In *Holiness Tracts Defending the Ministry of Women,* the testimony of various women preachers echoes some of these concerns while retaining primary emphasis on calling as a transforming event. Mrs. William E. Fisher described her call this way:

> When about fourteen years of age I was truly regenerated by the power of the Holy Ghost. Very soon after this I was impressed that God would have me spend my life in His vineyard in a special work. I had never heard of a woman preacher. Did not know that any woman had ever given her life to the work of the ministry. [after hearing a woman revivalist] After hearing the doctrine of sanctification preached as a second work of grace, I sought and obtained the experience by faith.—Acts 15:8, 9. Immediately the

21

call to God's work pressed upon me, and as never before I had the burden for lost souls. . . . I soon had providential openings for soul-saving work. I entered the pulpit with His commission to preach the Gospel and the anointing of the Spirit was upon me.[12]

Jarena Lee, a woman in the African Methodist Episcopal Church, responded forthrightly to her experience of divine call, saying, "no one will believe me." Though Bishop Richard Allen gave her permission to be an exhorter, she also sought to fulfill her call by marrying a minister.[13] In the same way, Mary Lee Cagle, ambivalent about the divine imperative placed on her, married a minister years before she was ordained by the Church of Christ. It was only after struggling in prayer during her husband's final illness and death that "God sanctified her wholly, thus fitting her to go out on the battlefield as an Evangelist to win souls," and Mary Lee Cagle began to preach. These testimonies bear out Jean Miller Schmidt's observation concerning Methodist laywomen of that era: that only inner divine conviction [that they were called] and love for souls prompted many otherwise timid women to exhort and pray aloud in public in nineteenth-century America.[14]

The call of one other preaching woman merits special mention because her words echo Finney's understanding of ministry's goal: bringing people to faith in Christ. Phoebe Palmer, who never applied for a license to preach, asserted:

That God has called me to stand before the people, and proclaim His truth, has long been beyond question. So fully has God made my commission known to my own soul, and so truly has He set His seal upon it, before the upper and lower world, in the conversion of thousands of precious souls, and the sanctification of a multitude of believers, that even Satan does not seem to question that my call is divine.[15]

The integrity of a call, in Palmer's theology, was not dependent on the manner in which it was apprehended, but rather the fruit borne by the work of the one called. Its authenticity was also not dependent on ecclesial sanction. She exhorted other women to obey God's call with these words: "And now, my dear sister, do not be startled, when I tell you that you have been ordained for a great work. Not by the imposition of mortal hands, or a call from man, no, Christ, the great Head of the church, hath chosen you, and 'ordained you, that ye should go and bring forth fruit.' ''[16]

What conclusions can be drawn about the way nineteenth- and early twentieth-century women perceived their calls to preach the gospel? First, the nature of call as discrete experience reflected a popular piety of the time that spoke about Christian initiation and growth in terms of conversion and sanctification. Though it would be overstatement to assert that this strain of Protestantism determined what ultimately happens at divine initiative, I believe it is fair to observe that the prevailing culture gave them what vocabulary they had to describe their calls to preach. For both men and women of the period, the sense of call to preach was often linked to another religious turning point or crisis experience.

A second conclusion is that a woman's sense of call legitimized a form of ministry even in churches that refused women a license to preach. Jarena Lee was accommodated as an "official traveling exhorter" by the A.M.E. Church, though the denomination's 1852 General Conference soundly defeated a resolution licensing women to preach. Third, the perception that they were called by God led to an increase in the number of nonaffiliated itinerant evangelists, as demonstrated in literature about Pentecostal and holiness women preachers.

A fourth characteristic of these early women preachers and their calls—in contrast to some contemporary mass media evangelists—is the absence of megalomania. Strong conviction accompanied by humility and sometimes a degree of self-deprecating humor appear regularly in their testimonies. Even Aimee Semple McPherson, in spite of her publicity stunts and notoriety, evokes smiles in describing the call to preach that came during a near-death experience: "Just before losing consciousness, as I hovered between life and death, came the voice of my Lord, so loud that it startled me: 'NOW WILL YOU GO?' And I knew it was 'Go,' one way or the other. . . . ''[17]

A final characteristic of these testimonies, just as significant as "event vs. process," is the sense that the call was perceived predominantly as one to preach, rather than to a ministry of word and sacrament. Had the understanding of ministry articulated by Finney been less weighted in favor of the pulpit, the issues confronting nineteenth-century women preachers might have been altered considerably. The conflict over ordination would have come to a head even sooner than it did.

RECURRENT THEMES AND THEOLOGICAL ISSUES

How much have things changed for the woman preacher since the days of Phoebe Palmer and Antoinette Brown? In some ways, the issues surrounding a woman's call to ministry have remained the same; women still identify a sense of vocation as a significant motivation for entering Christian ministry. A second recurrent theme in this survey is related to the first: a degree of uncertainty or tension concerning the woman preacher's relationship to the church. Nearly all the women expressed awareness that they would be perceived as "different" by clergy and laity, and the difference was often perceived as an obstacle to be negotiated. Third, the desire of contemporary women preachers to identify with particular nineteenth- and early twentieth-century women preachers was like the earlier tendency to look further back into the life of the church for historical precedent and/or biblical sanction for their ministry.

There are also significant *differences* between the calls of contemporary preaching women and those of a century ago. First, the majority of women today seek affiliation with established churches as opposed to operating independently or within a smaller sect. Most women who were willing to discuss the call to preach sought or were still seeking professional credentials within large, established churches. This is unlike the *modus operandi* of earlier women, who were less likely to exercise their ministry in mainline denominations.

A second difference is in the nature of the call. Contemporary women tend to describe an ongoing process, while earlier preachers talked about a life-changing event, sometimes simultaneous with conversion or sanctification. This is not surprising, given that mainline churches as a whole do not speak about conversion or sanctification as they did a century ago.

A third and very interesting difference is in women's defense of a call being challenged. The nineteenth-century woman preacher vindicated her ministry by pointing to evidence of the Holy Spirit's anointing, biblical precedent, the number of souls converted, and other empirical signs that her work was "bearing fruit." With the general decline in mainline churches today, few women (or men) preachers would dare use statistics in this way. A woman pursuing or practicing ordained ministry is more likely to appeal to (1) a contemporary sense of fairness: "women ought to have the same professional opportunities men have" or (2) the reasonableness of feminine leadership: "does gender matter, as long as the job gets done?" or (3) prophetic witness: "we're transforming the way people think about women and the Church" rather than more measurable results of her preaching.

Though these differences echo changes in the church as a whole, the understanding of call should not be reduced to a culturally-determined phenomenon. A variety of factors may help account for ways women presently speak about their vocation. In some instances, language about "rights" has replaced language about "call." More time is spent appealing for approval of a person or group's ministry on the grounds of justice rather than the argument that it is the divine will manifesting itself. For example, the Roman Catholic Church has recently allowed some married Episcopal priests to switch their affiliation and priesthood to the Catholic Church. In the subsequent controversy, many have asked why "new" priests have the right to be married, while those whose priesthood has always been Catholic aren't granted the same right. In other words, the argument has been less about whether these men were *called* to switch affiliation than about the *rights* of their colleagues.

In a similar vein, during a divinity school women's center meeting, students turned to a Catholic faculty member and asked, "Doesn't it bother you that as a woman you don't have the right to become a priest?" The professor paused and then replied, "Not at all; I am not called to the priesthood." We could argue the

25

adequacy of the response on the grounds that one woman's absence of call is not all women's; however, my purpose in citing the incident is to note the tendency among women (and men) today to mix the language and concept of rights with the language and concept of call.

An additional factor that may contribute to less specificity in contemporary women's calls to preach is ambiguity in the denominations that license or ordain them. It is expected that candidates for ministry be convinced of their calling, but catechetical literature and instruction material for ministerial candidates do not give much help to the woman who wonders if what she perceives *is* a call to ministry. Adding to the ambiguity is the degree of pluralism in large, mainline denominations. These churches are likely to be subject to regional and jurisdictional idiosyncrasies in interpreting instructions concerning candidacy.

For instance, when a friend of mine was a candidate for ordination, his mentor advised him, "for heaven's sake, *don't* tell the Board about the vision you had!" The mentor wanted to help the candidate anticipate theological biases operating in that place at that time. A woman or man entering the ministry must not only understand and fulfill the written requirements, but also hear the regional accent of the denomination deciding about her or his candidacy. Institutional guidelines are often broad and general; this allows for flexibility but also makes them vulnerable to manipulation.

Denominational guidelines agree that a candidate's inward call to ministry is important, but their primary focus is on the outward call: ministerial functions and responsibilities, understanding of vocation in the Reformed tradition, institutional testing and confirmation. In this respect they are reminiscent of the nineteenth-century testimonies, in which a woman preacher was vindicated by the results of her work (souls were being saved). The nineteenth-century woman, however, was more likely to work independently or in a small denomination with a strong social-cultural identity. Contemporary mainline denominations do not have this identity; they are more likely to take pride in their theological and cultural diversity. The attention given to outward call may reflect greater consensus about ministerial functions than about ministerial identity.

IMPLICATIONS FOR DISCUSSING THE CALL TO PREACH

There seems to be no argument that a call is necessary for Christian ministry, lay or ordained. Some regard baptism as a call to be a faithful servant in a Christian community, but this is not a call to assume the leadership role of preaching. Others give accounts of experiencing a specific call to preach at the time of their conversion/baptism.

In the nineteenth and early twentieth centuries, claiming a divine call did not eliminate the barriers to women's full participation in mainline churches. It did, however, spur women to act as agents of change and to search for avenues to express that sense of vocation. A woman's call served a number of functions in her life and ministry; it was her impetus to begin preaching, her refuge and solace when her ministry was challenged or rejected, and one way to account for the fruits of her labor. The ongoing struggle to practice ministry in the face of opposition served to heighten (and perhaps crystallize) her conviction that this was indeed God's will, whatever others might say. Her call was shared as testimony to edify and encourage others and often identified as a turning point in personal religious experience. Popular piety of the time was congenial to such testimony, even if it had questions about the propriety of letting the speaker have the floor.

The contemporary woman will find that mainline American Protestantism's self-image has changed along with its stance towards women's ordination. This will affect her inherited frame of reference for perceiving a divine call, the way it is discussed during her candidacy, and, perhaps, the ongoing role of call in her ministry and identity. A woman's sense of call continues to function as the main impetus for preaching and seeking ordination. It may also continue to be solace or rallying point in the face of religious bodies that resist or prohibit the ordination of women. The relative absence of discussion of one's calling in available sermons by women suggests that this kind of testimony is not expected by congregations, but it does not mean congregations would necessarily welcome or shun its inclusion. Most of the contemporary women who gave more details concerning their sense of vocation did not describe it as a major turning point in their lives, or link it to another religious experience.

A woman's call to preach is most likely to be a controversial issue in the process of candidacy for ordination early in her career, rather than occasional invitations to be guest preacher, or later in her career. If we assume that the candidate is sophisticated enough to discern the pluralism within a local church or her denomination, she will also be aware of the degree of tolerance or even relativism that must operate to hold the body together. This range of theological opinion means that the woman candidate will encounter questions, challenges (gender-related and otherwise), and support towards her call coming from a great variety of perspectives—all of which may have a vote. If she is one of a group of candidates under consideration, she may discover that there is no formal or informal consensus on what is a genuine inward call nor what outward fruits confirm it.

In the face of this, a woman may be tempted to become a theological chameleon, to rely solely on affirmative action to have its way with a board, or attempt to "set them straight" about ministry and/or the nature of Christian faith. A wiser strategy is to attend to the "language" spoken by those who are interviewing her, and use it to speak her convictions without compromising them. This is the method recommended by Paul in I Corinthians 9:19-23, and it is an interactive device preachers employ every time they speak to a new congregation. It respects the integrity of the listeners simultaneously with the truth claims of the message. In addition, women should be prepared to make a case for the "outward call" of the church, by noting previous leadership experience and current evidence suggesting that confirmation of her call would be a responsible decision. Taking these steps will not guarantee acceptance and ordination, but the candidate will be assured she has borne faithful and coherent witness to God's claim on her life, trusting the Spirit to equip her for the challenges that lie ahead.

Finally, a woman in ministry can reclaim some of the positive personal and pastoral functions that calling served for her foremothers. Keeping a journal may draw her attention to evidence that her ministry is bearing fruit, and reaffirm her conviction that ordained ministry is her vocation. Telling a congregation or church school class about the experiences that led to her decision for ministry may inspire others and enable them to recognize God's claim on their lives in a new way. It may also sensitize the preacher to the ongoing presence of Jesus Christ in her own life and in the community of faith.

*S*eeing another woman in the pulpit has the effect of raising a sort of mirror to the woman preacher. It causes her to compare her own work with this other person who is like her and yet not like her, to reflect on how she has grown and what she may become.

A feminine role model can demonstrate what a masculine one can only parody. The way a woman's laughter, solemnity, tension, and other moods come across over a public address system is something only a woman preacher can show another.

*W*hen a woman who is a role model testifies to the divine, enabling grace at work in her own life and ministry, her successors learn to claim its sustaining power for themselves.

T W O

ROLE MODELS AND THE WOMAN PREACHER

T he absence of female role models for women in ministry is occasionally lamented by contemporary seminarians. It is identified as one more indication of the pervasive sexism in the history and contemporary life of the church. One of my colleagues wryly commented on the opposite problem male seminarians experience: difficulty in developing their own method of preaching and ministry, due to constant comparison to other (male) pulpit stars. Evidence supporting my colleague's observation is manifested in introductory preaching classes. Now and then a male student will attempt to mirror the syntax, inflection, and/or gestures of a famous preacher he has heard. Even if he succeeds in this effort, he becomes only an imitation of someone else rather than genuinely himself. Women students, not making the same kind of identification with a male preacher, seem freer to develop their own gifts and styles.

A fairly small percentage of women studying for ministry have known or seen women doing what they are preparing to do. In a 1983 survey of 635 women in ministry, 46 percent identified another clergywoman as important to their decision to seek ordination in their denomination. However, 34 percent of the respondents didn't know a woman in ministry, or said the question did not apply to them.[1] In a case study of 838 United Methodist clergywomen, which began in 1979, the absence of role models

THE WOMAN IN THE PULPIT

and the ''superwoman syndrome'' were the two biggest problems women reported experiencing on the job.[2]

When I began studying women in ministry nearly ten years ago, half of those I interviewed had met a woman minister, but only 10 percent identified a woman among their role models. In addition to this, few of them knew when their denominations began ordaining women, or anything about the history that led to this event. They saw themselves as pioneers on a lonely and uncertain frontier. In more recent interviews with women students in the M.Div. program at Duke Divinity School, approximately 40 percent claimed they had at least one female role model before beginning their theological education. Although this reflects the sharp increase in the number of women entering ordained ministry in the last decade, it is still a very different situation from what men face as they envision their goals and style in the local church pulpit.

In this chapter, I survey the female role models most frequently named and lauded by women preachers, and describe their value and limitations. Next, I present what less well-known role models, male and female, do for the woman in the pulpit. Finally, I raise the question of what kinds of role models are currently in short supply for the woman preacher, and how this may affect her ministry.

PHOEBE, JULIAN, AND COMPANY: POPULAR ROLE MODELS AND THE WOMAN IN THE PULPIT

At a recent gathering of women administrators and seminary faculty, innovative worship experiences punctuated the end of each day's sessions. The liturgical moment that was most puzzling for me was when we were instructed to join hands and sing the following words to the tune of ''Jacob's Ladder'':

> We are dancing Sarah's circle,
> We are dancing Sarah's circle,
> We are dancing Sarah's circle,
> Sisters one and all.

I had read a variation of these lyrics as part of a "Croning Liturgy" in Rosemary Radford Ruether's *Women-Church*. In that instance, the participants sang, "We are casting Janet's circle . . . sisters all around" (Janet was the name of the woman being feted).³ But what could be made of "dancing Sarah's circle"? We were standing in a circle, but not moving. Nothing was said about Sarah in the rest of the service. I assumed the Sarah in question was the wife of Abraham, but could recall nothing in biblical tradition about her being associated with dancing or circles. Upon further reflection, I concluded that merely invoking the name of Sarah was understood as legitimizing the presence and role of women in faith-history.

The first function of popularly cited role models, then, is reminding women clergy (and those they serve) of the presence of women of the history of their faith. The significance of the woman whose name is invoked is not necessarily what she did or said, but what she symbolizes in the minds of those calling her to remembrance. Sarah, Miriam, Mary Magdalene, and, to a lesser extent, Mary the mother of Jesus, Hildegard of Bingen, and Joan of Arc normally serve an *iconic* function for the woman preacher. They may be valuable for the contemporary woman who feels relatively invisible or powerless in the church; she identifies with women of other eras whose names survived despite living in a patriarchal milieu. She may single out a particular virtue or image associated with the icon, and claim its presence in her own life: Sarah's laughter, Miriam's cleverness, Joan of Arc's courage, and so on.

In some instances, the woman cannot be more than a symbol, because little or nothing is known about her except her name; Persis, Junia, and Thecla are examples of this. More often, however, it is a matter of deeper knowledge not being needed for the symbol to "work" in the woman preacher's or the community's consciousness. The iconic function of these women in history is not limited to women in ministry, but may be more powerful for them because of the way it affirms their own self-understanding. Joan Chittister, O.S.B., describes this type of role model by saying, "The good news is that great women have always walked the earth . . . their footprints are still clear . . . their presence has changed things both in church and society.''[4]

The popular role model as ''icon'' does not have the explicit, discernible effect on women's preaching ministries that other role models do. This is because the role model is only a visual or aural reminder of women's presence: the life-history, struggles, and work of the woman in question are not explored in any depth. The preacher does not shape her message or method in preaching around the example set by the feminine forebear; singing about ''Sarah's circle,'' for example, was not related to anything in the homily that followed.

A second function of frequently invoked role models is *establishing precedent* for the woman preacher's calling, language, and efforts to challenge traditional patterns of ministry and understanding of the nature of the church. As noted in the first chapter, when women have been required to defend their call to ministry, it is common for them to name women from the New Testament or selected periods of church history as evidence that God does indeed call women to preach. Nineteenth-century evangelical women pointed to the precedent of the risen Christ commanding Mary Magdalene, ''go to my brethren and say to them. . . .'' After careful exegesis, they cited the example of Phoebe, a messenger commanded by Paul as a helper to him and to many.

In more recent controversies over the ministry and ordination of women, Ann Hutchinson, Antoinette Brown, Anna Howard Shaw, Isabel Carter Heyward and others have been named as examples of women who followed their calling despite fierce opposition. It is the example of their *lives*—their faithfulness and courage in the midst of struggle, rather than their *preaching method*, that is a model for women in the contemporary church. In the sermon excerpt that follows, a Baptist woman preaching on Judges 4:1-24 showed how one such model informed her ministry:

> In my ear now is the song of Deborah. It is a song of courage and
> power. A song of women interpreting the will of God, risking their

lives to do the will of God. It is a song of shattered role expectations. It is a song that breaks the rules that justice may be done. . . . It is a song that reminds me that I am sometimes afraid to sing. For it is hard to sing the song of Deborah, especially if I must sing it alone.[5]

Liturgies as well as sermons demonstrate the relationship between "precedents" and "present company." Consider this portion of Miriam Therese Winter's feminist liturgy, "Valiant Women":

LEADER: Let us now praise valiant women recalling to life representatives of all those unsung heroines whose lives are living testimony that God is God in us.
ALL: We praise valiant women, whose lives give hope to us. . . .
LEADER: Mary Fisher, missionary, Quaker, who dared preach publicly at Cambridge, England, in front of the college gate in 1653 . . . All women in ministry, ordained and unordained, all who were first to pave the way and all who followed after:
ALL: Hail, valiant women![6]

The "valiant women" called to remembrance are not "icons" in this context, for sufficient biographical information is given for the women to serve as precedent for women to imitate them in specific ways. Some preachers and worship leaders go beyond naming heroines of the faith as precedent or encouragement for their own ministry. They are used as examples to the entire church. In the following sermon excerpt, listeners of both sexes were exhorted to challenge attitudes and practices that compromise faithful discipleship:

Mary of Bethany responded to Jesus in faith and entered into a right and proper relationship with God. She anointed Jesus' feet with costly perfume and wiped them with her hair. She gave her all to her beloved Lord in her unorthodox fashion. She was a woman of faith and an example to each of us. May God empower us with God's Spirit that we may challenge the prevailing attitudes of our day that quench God's Spirit.[7]

Popular role models also serve as precedent for the language women use in preaching. This is different from searching for scriptural precedent for using one word rather than another; instead, it is a particular woman credited with coining a term or phrase. The one perhaps most often cited for the use of feminine language about God is Julian of Norwich. In *Revelations of Divine Love,* the Motherhood of God is expressed in the second Person of the Trinity: "Jesus Christ, who doeth good against evil, is our very Mother . . . As truly as God is our Father, so truly is God our Mother."[8]

Feminist theologians build upon Julian's work (among others) as a model for articulating the feminine aspects of the divine nature. Julian's use of language becomes justification for their own liturgical and homiletical experiments. One reservation I have about using *Revelations of Divine Love* as precedent for the feminization of the Trinity is an analogy Julian draws between "lower, sensual nature" and the feminine attributes of God: "For of God's making we are double: that is to say, substantial and sensual. Our substance is that *higher* [italics mine] part which we have in our Father, God, almighty. And the second Person of the Trinity is our Mother . . . in taking on our sensuality."[9]

Though a preacher may emulate Julian by using a balance of feminine and masculine language about divinity, she may unintentionally perpetuate patriarchy by recapitulating the hierarchical valuation of God's dual nature. A sermon by Carter Heyward shows one way maternal and other feminine language about divinity is incorporated into preaching:

> . . . the Holy One of Israel, whom Jesus called abba (daddy) and who, in truth, is also the Mother of us all . . . Only the eyes of faith are able to see what Paul calls "the secret and ancient wisdom of God"—the fact that the Divine Presence seldom has much to do with the "good order" of religion and society. She has rather everything to do with the inclusion of those whom the custodians of good order have cast out because they are the wrong color, culture, creed, class.[10]

Role models do more than legitimate "new" or unfamiliar language about divinity. Women preachers in recent years have looked to activities and experiences normally associated with women as a source of language for their preaching. Twenty years ago it was uncommon to hear sermons that alluded to childbirth, baking bread, keeping house, and nurturing children. With the advent of preachers for whom these represent everyday life (and who wish to honor their mothers' discipleship lived out through these tasks), a new vocabulary has been incorporated into pulpit discourse.

The "icon" and "precedent" functions are two ways in which popular role models serve contemporary women preachers. But there are limitations to the value of such role models. They do not shape the woman's style of preaching, except for encouraging her to use language she may not have heard male clergy use. The role model as precedent for action may help a woman persist as she pursues education, ordination, and appointment/call to a local church. It is the local, less-known role model, however, who is apt to have some impact on the way a woman's pulpit style develops.

LOCAL ROLE MODELS AND THE WOMAN IN THE PULPIT

Among the women I have interviewed over the years, only one has named qualities of a *famous* preacher as something she wished to emulate; a black Baptist woman said Harry Emerson Fosdick was a role model for her because of the way he spoke to real human problems in the course of his preaching.[11] It is more common for women to speak of people they know personally as role models. Some of those surveyed focused on preaching per se, but often they talked about personal qualities or ministerial activities other than what was done in the pulpit. They identified both men and women as role models. Fathers who were pastors or college teachers, college chaplains and other clergy were the male role models named. Interview subjects who discussed preaching by these men spoke of their admiration for homiletical methods that transcend gender differences. A priest whose preaching was "very intelligent, very professional, and very pastoral—who also supports women in ministry'' was lauded by a Catholic seminary student. Another woman spoke of a Presbyterian minister whose sermons were "pastoral, and knowledgeable of doctrine.''[12] Gender issues were identified as part of male role models' preaching by only one woman, who was serving as a priest in the Church of Sweden. She described her childhood pastor's positive example in this way:

> I greatly admired the way he preached the Gospel. His style was not dominating or overbearingly masculine. His manner was mild, and yet it communicated authority when he spoke. He talked the language of the people. Occasionally he had his own doubts in faith, and he allowed this to show in his preaching.[13]

Even this assessment does not suggest that the woman had to "sort through" various aspects of a male pastor's style in order to claim those attributes that would be of value to her as a woman. In identifying specific methods worthy of emulation, gender does not seem to be a crucial factor for women choosing role models. Author and clergywoman Martha Kriebel noted that one reason ordained men served as effective role models for her was that they did not raise gender issues as a barrier to her pursuing similar ministry in the church.[14]

Gender was not the focal issue in descriptions of female role models given by interview subjects. The women preachers they admired were good storytellers, had a central theme or motif to the sermon, and used poetry well. They were praised for their ability to relate empathically while preaching, to present different levels of interpretation, for speaking clearly and conveying confidence. These qualities are not the exclusive property of women preachers, however. Female seminarians and ministers identified qualities they wanted to cultivate, rather than making a simpler identification with or rejection of a potential role model solely on the basis of gender. In the same way, other ministerial tasks or qualities that were extolled in women models were not expressly gender-oriented. A woman district superintendent was admired for being very assertive and intentional but yet sensitive to personal relationships in Christ. Two other women were praised for their "ministry of presence."

This suggests that for the task of preaching, women are able to find and seek to emulate models regardless of the preacher's gender. The "icon" or "precedent" may give her the courage to do what she may not have seen another woman do, but positive male role models can demonstrate good preaching method in the same way that positive female role models do. I believe the greater need for feminine role models, therefore, lies in two related but slightly different aspects of ministry.

ROLE MODELS NEEDED BY WOMEN IN THE PULPIT

The first kind of role model I want to suggest women preachers lack may strike the reader as a contradiction both of "models" and of what was said earlier about admired preaching methods transcending gender issues. Women clergy suffer from a shortage of opportunities to see and hear other women preaching. It is true women can appreciate and learn from male role models, yet their homiletical development would be enhanced by exposure to a greater range of preaching styles and methods *as manifested by women*. They are often deprived of the chance to identify other women as role models.[15]

Seeing another woman in the pulpit has the effect of raising a sort of mirror to the woman preacher. It causes her to compare her own work with this other person who is like her and yet not like her, to reflect on how she has grown and what she may become. For example, when I was twenty years old, I preached for the first time: a midweek Lenten service at my home church. It was more than four years later that I first heard another woman preach (in a local church rather than seminary classroom). The experience of listening to her address a small congregation in Manchester, England, had greater pedagogical value than I ever anticipated. I was far more attuned to this preacher's way of engaging the congregation, her inflection patterns and syntax, the way the acoustics of the sanctuary worked against her, than I was when male colleagues addressed the same congregation. It was not simply a matter of learning *from* Sister Mabel Sykes or looking for a vindication of women's call to proclaim the gospel: I was learning about myself as a preacher. Seeing another woman in the pulpit helped equip me for intentional homiletical development and the identification of potential problems in my own preaching.

Some of the things women can learn only by seeing and hearing other women in the pulpit may impress the reader as too prosaic to merit mention, yet they are important for effective preaching and leadership of worship. Listening to a male preacher, or to a recording of herself, will not inform a clergywoman of how a woman's voice, normally higher pitched than a man's, carries or is distorted by the worship space in which she normally preaches. Only being present to hear another woman in the pulpit will do that.

In our culture women normally wear makeup in public; men do not. How do distance and special lighting affect the appearance of a woman as she preaches? How can she avoid looking either "theatrical" or washed-out (either of which can disrupt effective communication)? Seeing another woman will give her the answer and enable her to make wise decisions. In nearly every culture, there are some gestures and body language that seem the exclusive property of each gender; how does feminine body language "work" when a woman is preaching? A feminine role model can demonstrate what a masculine one can only parody. The way a woman's laughter, solemnity, tension, and other moods come across over a public address system is something only a woman preacher can show another.

These are ways in which feminine role models help the woman preacher at a subconscious level. They also assist her in more deliberate ways. In the fourth chapter of this book, on self-disclosure, I discuss the way a woman in the pulpit may be perceived by the congregation as "representing" all women during the worship service. This representative function is also operating for other clergywomen who hear her. The woman preacher's appropriation of denominational and cultural tradition (and/or her critique of it) reveal to the novice preacher how such treatment of the subject matter sounds—and is heard—when coming from a woman's lips. The observant preacher will attend to the woman's manner of relating to the congregation during worship. She may ask herself how sex-role expectations or the preacher's explicit feminism shape the interaction, nurturing or thwarting it. She will make decisions about her own mode of interaction based on what she sees.

The second function for which women preachers need role models is for mentoring. After the "icon" and "precedent" models have done their work in encouraging a woman to claim God's call to ministry, feminine mentors help her to weigh various priorities and courses of action that confront any person in ministry. A relationship with a mentor is far more common for men in the early stages of their career than for women. In denominations with "supervising elders" or official advisory relationships using other nomenclature, males are more likely to have genuinely constructive (and comfortable) relationships than women. This is not necessarily because of ill will on the part of the predominantly male hierarchy, but rather because a man cannot be an example of a "successful," balanced woman in ministry.[16]

The absence of feminine mentors has been a problem for women entering many fields. In the early 1970s, when Gail Sheehy interviewed young career women about mentor relationships, she found most didn't know what she was talking about.[17] Female mentors were even less common, and it is reasonable to suppose that a similar pattern would be found among women in ordained ministry. A very small percentage of clergy in mainline denominations at that time were women, and even fewer had reached positions of seniority and power where they were able to serve as advocates as well as models for other women. With the advent of affirmative action policies, the church has more women serving as seminary professors, district superintendents, heads of boards and agencies, and bishops. There are still relatively few women serving pastoral appointments as senior pastors in multi-staff churches or sole pastors of fairly large churches, however, and for women coming up through seminary, these are more immediate, accessible, and helpful role models.

A recent seminary graduate gave voice to still another concern about women as mentors. At a continuing education event, she said to a small group:

> Whenever I don't see how I'm going to get a sermon ready for next Sunday, or frankly feel like throwing in the towel, I think about Nancy. I mean, there she is with one child in kindergarten and another in diapers, a husband who's busy with his own job, and a building program under way—and she never seems to lose it! I tell myself if Nancy can do it, maybe I can do it.

The more experienced pastor, without being aware of it, modeled for another woman how to balance the numerous and often conflicting demands of ministry—equated here with preparing a sermon—and family life. While men also need role models for these tasks, the presence of mentors is particularly essential for women whose earlier feminine mentors faced a different set of challenges and inherited cultural expectations.

Women of their mothers' generation sought to balance family commitments and faithful discipleship as they supported their husbands' ministries, ran church suppers and rummage sales, sang in the choir and taught Sunday school. Some of them were employed outside the home as well, but it was understood that a Christian woman's commitment was primarily to her family's needs; they took precedence over all other endeavors. This role model is not a "bad" one, but it does not match the obligations of contemporary ordained ministry; nor does it match the living situation of a strikingly high percentage of women in full-time Christian service today. To put it another way, the congregation expects the preacher to lead worship and present a sermon on Sunday morning, regardless of her husband's business trip, her child's measles, or her aging parents' demands on her time the previous week. These issues are addressed in the third chapter, on preaching and parish ministry, though it is beyond the scope of this book to present a comprehensive treatment of the family life of women ministers.

IMPLICATIONS FOR WOMEN PREACHERS SEEKING OR BECOMING ROLE MODELS

Though positive role models are useful for theological, professional, and personal maturation of anyone in ministry, a general shortage of feminine models means that a woman must be intentional about identifying and claiming those who will help equip and sustain the maturation process. Because models serve differing functions at various stages of ministry, the woman preacher will also do well to discern which ones are needed at a given time, which have outlived their usefulness, and which, if not set aside, may actually impede her development. In this respect, women and men share a common hazard: the danger of over-identification with a model at the expense of one's individual integrity and gifts.[18]

A woman considering ministry may be impelled by circumstances to find "icon" role models. Discovery of the presence and work of women in the church in ages past may serve to clarify the Holy Spirit's claim of her life, and enable her to articulate her call to ministry from within a sense of community rather than in isolation. Reminders of the place of women in salvation history may be incorporated into liturgy, preaching, and the education program of the church, thus affirming the divine worth of all in the contemporary community of faith. These models are a reminder of the communion of saints. Awareness of them militates against exclusive thinking on the part of the church, or narcissism and/or a sense of isolation on the part of the woman responding to God's inward call to preach.

A woman preacher should study and claim "precedent" role models to familiarize herself with the theological grounds for prophetic witness. They are useful both at the beginning of ministry, as they impart confidence for risk-taking, and later on, when the staying power of forerunners in ministry will encourage the woman preacher to remain faithful to her call. The stories of these role models should also be shared with local church congregations; they sensitize the church to the contextual nature of ministry, as well as challenging prejudices. They may even be examined as "case studies" for resolving problems in the local congregation.

"Local role models" are valuable to both women and men in achieving competency at the task of preaching. Homiletical method often transcends gender; a lucid and engaging proclamation in itself is neither male nor female. Women looking for ways to improve their preaching should not automatically discount the pedagogical value of observing effective communication strategies practiced by male preachers simply because they cannot provide *feminine* models. In addition to the good example a local role model can supply, he or she can often provide feedback for the one seeking to incorporate the skills presented by the model. The possibility for interaction and critique may facilitate the preacher's growth and help her identify her own gifts for proclamation.

Finally, a woman preacher should seek out opportunities to listen to other women in the pulpit, even if she is comfortable with her own style and has received positive feedback from her congregation. Feminine role models provide a much-needed mirror for women preachers, so that they obtain a sense of what their congregations experience in listening to a feminine rather than a masculine voice from the pulpit. Regular experiences of listening to other women preach help a clergywoman pinpoint particular aspects of her own homiletical method that need attention and, perhaps, modification. In addition, such experiences clarify for preacher and congregation the relationship between gender expectations (among other expectations) and their theology of worship.

Women who have been in ministry for years have a responsibility to those coming up through the ranks. Given the perceived resistance to the novelty of hearing a woman preach and lead worship, and the feminine tendency to assume responsibility/blame if all is not well in preacher-congregation relationships, seasoned pastors can reassure novices that they are not alone, without advocates, or the first to struggle with these issues. In a culture where patterns of family life have changed significantly since the end of World War II, but where the church may preserve nostalgic expectations of what women are expected to do and not do, role models can warn other women against the "superwoman" syndrome. This is done by being accessible to other women preachers (and also laywomen in the church), and by being candid, but not pessimistic, about her own struggles. When a woman who is a role model testifies to the divine, enabling grace at work in her own life and work, her successors learn to claim its sustaining power for themselves.

*H*owever one chooses to define authority, it appears that women identify and claim it more readily in the ministries of word and sacrament than in the ministry of "order" (parish leadership and administration).

*[O*ne] factor supporting clergywomen's greater comfort in leading worship than in engaging in other pastoral work may operate unconsciously. Though she doesn't think about it constantly, a woman preacher may safely assume that she will not be interrupted, shouted down, patronized, or otherwise visually or audibly challenged during worship.

*C*oncern for equilibrium in the pastor-congregation relationship may make a woman preacher reluctant to use power in a legitimate, but perhaps confrontational way. Women are affirmed for interacting as mediators and nurturers in the church—roles which have been modeled by generations of ministers' wives, deaconesses, and savvy church secretaries.

THREE

CLAIMING AND EXERCISING AUTHORITY

A curious paradox often operates among contemporary women clergy and their denominations. For generations, the church allowed women to engage in many aspects of pastoral ministry, but prohibited them from preaching or "priestly" ministry. Individual congregations are still more likely to resist the idea of a woman leading public worship than taking other leadership roles in the life of the church. Women are well aware of this opposition. Yet in the present day, when nearly all mainline denominations in North America do ordain women, many women say they are *more* comfortable preaching and celebrating the sacraments than exercising authority/leadership in other parochial duties. One American Baptist woman preacher summed up her ambivalence this way: "How do I understand my authority? Wow! That's wild! Normally I'm a real Caspar-ina Milquetoast, but when I'm in the pulpit, I am IN CHARGE!!"[1] A United Methodist seminarian confessed she felt very inadequate and unsure about authority issues, but in the pulpit, she counted on good preparation to give her authority. "Credibility" seemed to be used as a synonym for authority by this woman. More recently, a Lutheran woman I interviewed voiced a contrasting opinion on authority issues and the pulpit:

> I think [authority] is a big issue for women. Part of what I have noticed is that women aren't as comfortable taking on the role of

47

authority necessary in the pulpit and their image suffers with the congregation. Or they are more comfortable with admitting uncertainty and are poorly evaluated by the congregation as a result.

It is evident that the word *authority* is used by women preachers to mean different things. For the Baptist clergywoman I quoted first, authority was equated with being "in charge"—with exercising power equal to or greater than those around her. For other women, authority means having demonstrated the credibility or competence to lead. In her book on feminist ministry, author Lynn Rhodes suggested the word itself evokes ambivalence among women. This is because women equate authority with their experiences of church hierarchies. They associate the term with male-defined theology, and with those who have used the "authority" of the Bible and church history to demonstrate why women should not be ordained.[2] In a similar manner, Christine Smith's feminist paradigm for preaching calls into question the way authority is traditionally understood and used:

> Authority in preaching has traditionally been defined as that quality of proclamation that pertains to special rights, power, knowledge, and capacity to influence or transform . . . [From a feminist perspective,] preaching is not so much a matter of the right and privilege of the position with all its distinctive power; rather it is a craft of authenticity weaving together mutuality, solidarity, and deeper faith sharing. . . . authority and intimacy are of necessity inextricably woven together in feminist preaching.[3]

Smith's critique finds expression in the ministries of those who eschew the word authority, and speak of their work in terms of responsibility, leadership, enabling, and so on. These are words that draw attention to a relationship of mutuality between parties, and the process of engaging in specific activities. Attention is drawn away from power as a possession or property of a person or group. Still other feminists categorize types of power/authority in terms of who exercises it: traditional authority, which has been assigned to an elite male group; charismatic authority, which is intrinsic to human interaction; and legal rational authority, which is the sharing of official power with those formerly shut out.[4] Clergywomen with this frame of reference identify charismatic authority as the type to which women most easily have access.

However one chooses to define authority, it appears that women identify and claim it more readily in the ministries of word and sacrament than in the ministry of "order" (parish leadership and administration). What is it about preaching and leading worship that causes ordained women less ambivalence and uncertainty than exercising authority in other aspects of ministry? In the pages that follow, reasons for this discrepancy are explored, and strategies are suggested for helping the woman preacher develop both confidence and competence in the leadership to which God has called her.

WOMEN'S "AUTHORITY" IN WORSHIP

I said earlier that women enjoy preaching and leading worship. Most feel they are doing a competent and effective job on Sunday morning. This is demonstrated in the data provided by the 635 women surveyed for *Women of the Cloth;* 97 percent of the clergywomen questioned evaluated themselves as "very effective" or "quite effective" in this area of their work.[5] The Episcopal clergywomen featured in *Women of the Word* spoke about their experiences as preachers in positive and enthusiastic terms; "marvelous" and "wonderful" were two adjectives used. Furthermore, the sheer volume of feminist liturgical materials versus feminist "administrative strategies" being published suggests that clergywomen are confident in the quality and integrity of their efforts in the former area of ministry.

The first source of women preachers' confidence—or comfort with exercising authority—was discussed in the opening chapter of this book on the question of call. In Protestant America, a "vocation" has often been understood as a call to preach/evangelize in public worship. A high percentage of the women who participated in the ATS survey registered a sense of divine call as their strongest motivation for pursuing a seminary education. It is not surprising, then, that their conviction would find expression in preaching and leading worship. Women I interviewed expressed the relationship this way:

> [My authority] comes from my call to be in the ministry of Word and Sacrament. My role is to be a vessel more than anything else. . . . My authority comes from God, who is using me [in worship].[6]
>
> I am aware of my inadequacies . . . yet I justify being in the pulpit because it was not my idea in the first place; it was God's.[7]

Closely related to the authority that comes from being persuaded that she is divinely called is the denomination's sanction of that call. Ordination is, among other things, the institution's affirmation that the woman candidate may indeed preach and celebrate the sacraments. One woman put it this way: "My authority comes from God in that I was called to preach, and it has been confirmed by the church in ordination." The "traditional rational" and legal-rational authorities legitimate a woman's leadership of discrete activities that members of her sex were previously prohibited from doing. With those kinds of power supporting her work, it is understandable that a woman preacher claims and uses the authority they give her. This is likely to be true even if she is critical of the way these power structures exist and function. If her denomination's polity is episcopal, such as in The United Methodist Church, the woman preacher may experience an even greater sense of security and confidence in her role as preacher and celebrant; after all, the most vehemently misogynic congregation cannot vote her out of the pulpit.

The next source of authority (or legitimacy) for the woman preacher is not necessarily gender-related. As hinted at earlier, the clergyperson leading worship is more comfortable with taking a leadership role when he or she is adequately prepared. One American Baptist clergywoman said that having thought a lot about her sermon subject, along with her own interpretation and insights, gave her credibility in the pulpit. Proving that they have done their homework gives confidence to preachers who are just beginning their ministry. For women, well-documented biblical and theological foundations may be required to justify their *presence* as well as give credence to their message.

This factor raises the stakes in adequate preparation as a source of authority. As one woman seminarian wryly commented, "Women have to be better than men to be considered okay or just possibly equal." This sort of works righteousness is a mixed blessing for women preachers. On the positive side, it is a legitimate and self-directed method of establishing one's credibility—in the pulpit or in other work. It is attained through measurable efforts on the part of the preacher. It promotes biblical literacy among clergy and laity, and suggests a high regard for the authority of the Bible. Many worshiping communities will applaud this. On the negative side, over-reliance on proof of preparation for authority reinforces cultural prejudices against the credibility of personal experience and conviction.

This is the kind of bias that allowed the apostles to discount the resurrection witness of Mary Magdalene; after all, she had no rabbinical training and couldn't document what she had seen at the empty tomb. If, as some feminist writers maintain, the starting point of a woman's sense of authority is honoring the validity of her own experience, a clergywoman may feel conflicted about pointing to an external source that devalues such experience.[8]

Another factor supporting clergywomen's greater comfort in leading worship than in engaging in other pastoral work may operate unconsciously. Though she doesn't think about it constantly, a woman preacher may safely assume that she will not be interrupted, shouted down, patronized, or otherwise visually or audibly challenged during worship. Even in those churches where verbal interaction between preacher and congregation is an integral part of worship, ushers, "nurses," or other delegated officers prevent disruptive demonstrations by worshipers. The relational expectations in worship are fairly clear; only one person preaches a sermon. The same person may celebrate the Eucharist and/or lead the rest of the liturgy, or that person may appoint qualified others to lead portions of the service. Congregations expect that someone is in charge of the service, and though they may disapprove of the person given that charge, they will not debate it during worship. The pastor-parishioner relationship may be evolving constantly during worship, but it occurs at the pastor's initiative. It is almost always safe for the woman preacher to assume that those in the pews will not challenge her leadership while the Sunday service is in progress. This cannot help but lend her some security as she engages in this aspect of her work.

Closely related to the woman preacher's position of strength and confidence while leading worship is the congregation's simultaneous security with the liturgy. A worship service has boundaries they may depend on: time limits, tacit understanding of what may and may not occur there, and a consensus of what constitutes "good worship" in a given denomination. The knowledge of boundaries enables worshipers to endure the leadership of someone whose credibility they otherwise doubt, for they can identify the beginning and ending of this religious activity. For example, a woman preacher who runs overtime or imposes a radically different order of worship will meet with more immediate and palpable resistance on Sunday morning than one who says things in her sermon the congregation does not like. Why? Because the first preacher has trespassed the "boundaries" of worship and deprived the congregation of that security. The second preacher has only tested the congregation's ability to honor mutually held role expectations in worship.

Finally, women preachers may experience a more comfortable sense of their authority leading worship than in other ministerial duties because it is, in one sense, a solo act. They relate to others present as priest/prophet/pastor to congregation, or choreographer before God, but other roles and relationships are not explicitly being presented. To put it simply, the person up front is not there by virtue of being next-door neighbor, spouse, precinct captain, or blood relative; she is there as preacher/worship leader. Even though the incidence of clergy couples is on the increase, very few ministers regularly lead worship as husband-wife or parent-child teams. They are not, therefore, expected to act out of those relationships while preaching. One clergywoman hinted at this while discussing her understanding of authority: "I don't think much about my authority. I feel so free—not self-conscious—

while I'm preaching. Not thinking about being a woman, or younger than a lot of folks there, or about my accent. It's like I'm just lifted up! And it's the Holy Spirit speaking through me and not me speaking the words.''

It may be that the perceived "separateness" of ordination liberates a woman preaching from the imposition of other role expectations that are more familiar to the congregation. At a church picnic, for example, a woman preacher may be expected to say grace, but she's also expected to bring a dish to pass, sit with her husband, and keep track of her children. It is likely she is expected *not* to be the only woman in the baseball game after the meal. The constellation of relationships and activities that may be imposed on a clergywoman in other contexts do not operate in worship. Her credibility and authority are not weighed against successful fulfillment of these other roles.

WOMEN'S "AUTHORITY" IN PARISH MINISTRY

In the previous paragraphs I have tried to account for the relative comfort women preachers report in exercising the ministry of word and sacrament. They are convinced that God has called them into this work, and are generally confident in their competence to preach and lead worship. Where unsureness about authority is voiced, it is often attributed to the preacher's youth, lack of experience or skills, or the nature of authority itself.

Women express less confidence and enthusiasm about other aspects of their work in the local church. When managing the budget, organizing a church staff, recruiting workers, etc., the authority needed is a different type from that which is exercised in worship. Leadership styles vary according to individual personality and congregation. The pastor's voice is not the only voice to be heard, as is the case in preaching. Even taking these differences into account, however, women do not see themselves as credible or competent to exercise authority here as they do in worship. For example, the *Women of the Cloth* survey revealed that only 44 percent of the women surveyed saw themselves as effective or quite effective at managing the church budget; 73 percent claimed that level of competence at organizing or motivating the paid staff; 58 percent thought they did well at stimulating parishioners to engage in service to others outside the church.[9] This is significantly lower than the 97 percent who saw themselves as effective worship leaders.

One reason for women's lack of confidence in their authority may be attributed to North American Protestantism's orientation toward the pulpit. As mentioned in chapter 1, women who claim a "call" to ministry tend to think of it in terms of preaching and leading worship. A strong sense of divine imperative sustains their vision of vocation. Unlike traditional Roman Catholics, Protestants do not generally associate other careers and tasks in terms of "calling." Therefore, the woman preacher and the church lack a sense of connection between the authority "bestowed" in call (and ordination) and the executive and other administrative work required of clergy.

This is illustrated by one woman preacher's account of a time of unrest in a congregation she served as associate pastor. Though there was strong support for her preaching and little objection to her leadership of worship, a congregational survey yielded comments such as "We need a young girl running this church like we need another hole in our heads!" The congregation did not see a correlation between ordination's authorizing leadership of worship and leadership in other ministries.

A second way to account for unease about exercising leadership skills outside of worship is related to women's "fear of success." In 1976 Gail Sheehy wrote about the inner conflict college women experienced concerning achievement. She attributed it partly to the fear that no one will marry a woman if she's too successful and independent, but also to a woman's socialization to nurture and defer to others.[10] Though some of Sheehy's writing is dated, I believe her observation about the culture's expectations of feminine behavior has implications for the clergywoman in the local church.[11] The average layperson does not want to compete with the minister for pulpit time, but there may be competition for dominance in other areas of church work.

A Presbyterian clergywoman's story demonstrates this issue.

After several years in seminary administration, Ann became pastor of a small, rural church. Controversy arose over the church budget. The congregation never had a stewardship plan for benevolences and missions. The church treasurer decided how all money was spent; the deacons and session didn't challenge him. Ann, who knew both church polity and sound financial management, insisted on a budget and on the treasurer relinquishing his monopoly on church funds, but it didn't happen without a struggle. The treasurer called her "a dumb woman" and said he didn't need her interference in keeping the books. Resolution was a painful process: more than a question of good bookkeeping, it was heightened by a woman's competence threatening a man's. Though competition for leadership of some aspect of church life is an issue for male clergy as well, challenges to their authority are not based on gender. It is not surprising that women report lack of confidence in their effective leadership here.

A third way to account for a woman preacher's comparative diffidence in administration reflects feminist psychologists' observation that feminine identity is awakened, established, and nurtured in the context of relationships (as opposed to masculine identity being rooted more in achievements.)[12] Concern for equilibrium in the pastor-congregation relationship may make a woman preacher reluctant to use power in a legitimate, but perhaps confrontational way. Women are affirmed for interacting as mediators and nurturers in the church—roles that have been modeled by generations of ministers' wives, deaconesses, and savvy church secretaries. These forebears wielded a degree of indirect or charismatic power, based on mutual support networks and the authority of their husbands/employers—but it was power *with* rather than *over* others when decisions were made. A woman interviewed for *Clergy Women and Their Worldviews* described the tension she felt between maintaining relationships and dealing with conflict:

[Men] can and do get angry. They always show strength. Anger is a big issue. . . . Women can't get angry . . . don't know how. . . . People can't deal with it when they do. . . . It's important to me to be sensitive and attuned to problems; I'm just not tuned in right now to career. . . .[13]

The author who interviewed this woman preacher drew this conclusion about women's reluctance to claim "legal-rational" or "traditional" authority:

> As women, socially accustomed to a status subordinate to that of men, there is substantial appeal for them in the idea of peer networks in social organization, compared with hierarchies. . . . They seem neither psychologically nor ideologically prepared to lead from a high position of dominance and control over others. Ambivalence on this score is exceptional among the informants [who participated in the study].[14]

The disinclination of many clergywomen, particularly younger ones, to claim legitimate authority in dealing with other authorities—leading a congregation through everyday tasks, or confronting an actual conflict in the church—takes its toll on them. Combined with the feminine tendency to take responsibility/blame for maintaining equilibrium in relationships, it can lead to depression, feelings of helplessness, and vocational discouragement. It may also result in a schizophrenic approach to ministry; anger and frustration get played out in the pulpit or personal life, rather than being allowed expression elsewhere.

I have found this pattern repeated periodically among women in seminary. Frustration over someone using exclusive language at chapel services is a regular topic at their weekly support group meetings. Yet women choose to boycott chapel, complain among themselves, and/or occasionally model inclusiveness when asked to lead worship, rather than directly address the persons using offensive language. Calling another student or professor to accountability is, for them, a too-frightening exercise of their own power. I do not mean to suggest that this particular pattern is the norm for all women in seminary and ministry, but in our culture women *are* characteristically socialized to subjugate their own authority for the sake of preserving peace. Where a male pastor is praised for being a strong leader, a female pastor using the same method is criticized for being pushy, too aggressive, and unfeminine. It is small wonder that clergywomen tend to believe they are less effective when taking administrative responsibility.

A final way to account for women's gravitation toward liturgical rather than parochial leadership is political. It has more to do with traditional (male) hierarchy and changing configurations of ministry than with the question of women's confidence. It pertains to the nature of diaconal ministry in relationship to the offices of presbyter and bishop. Long before women were ordained by most denominations, deaconess orders were means of living out a calling to be in ministry. Deaconesses describe their work as a "calling," just as women in ordained ministry are prone to do. Though the work of deaconess can vary considerably according to time and place, they are usually involved in education, social work, nursing, missionary, and evangelistic endeavors. The job description of a deaconess can also look remarkably like that of director of Christian education or parish assistant in a local church. Deaconesses exercise *limited* authority and answer to a bishop, superintendent, pastor, or judicatory board.[15]

The number of women in deaconess orders and some denominational social service agencies declined significantly after World War II, but especially during the 1960s. This is the period when increasing numbers of women entered ordained ministry. Ordination gave them access to the authority to preach and celebrate the sacraments (though in some denominations deaconesses occasionally did the former, they were never authorized to do the latter). I believe it has also resulted in a disassociation from the kinds of leadership women had exercised earlier. Exercising the authority to which deaconesses had access is unconsciously associated with being barred from other types of authority.

For example, among seminary women, there is sometimes a resistance toward field education assignments and pastoral appointments with minimal opportunities for preaching and leading worship, but maximum involvement in Christian education, youth work, and routine parish administration. For these women, authority exercised in such ministries is second-class rank with a second-class salary and benefits package (which was certainly the case for deaconesses in years past). It may be accompanied by concern that leadership here is a ''dead end'' that will not advance their careers. Elsie Gibson, who conducted one of the early case studies of women in ordained ministry, suggested that the administrative and educational tasks delegated by (male) senior pastors in multi-staff churches are seen as carrying inferior status.[16] Therefore, for some clergywomen discomfort with exercising authority in parish concerns may not be based on feelings of incompetence, but on the underlying suspicion that this power is not worth having.

IMPLICATIONS FOR WOMEN IN PULPIT AND PARISH

Not all women preachers have difficulty claiming and exercising authority outside the Sunday worship service. However, extensive studies of women in ministry demonstrate that a significant percentage see themselves as less effective in parish administration than preaching. In addition, clergywomen are subject to gender-related expectations and criticism that are not brought to bear on clergymen. A single paradigm for leadership would not do justice to the differing tasks of ministry, nor to the diversity of gifts in women called to ministry. What strategies, then, will help the woman preacher develop both competence and confidence in the work God has called her to do?

A first step is learning to hear criticism based solely on gender as a commentary on the critic more than on the preacher herself. Cultivating a sense of humor can often expose sexism for what it is without escalating the conflict. It also reveals the difference between criticism that can ultimately help a preacher's effectiveness (''her pulpit voice is too shrill'') and accusations that only reflect the speaker's insecurities (''she's just a dumb woman''). For instance, during my first year of teaching, a male student took it upon himself to give me a midterm evaluation. With all seriousness he told me, ''Most people in your class think you're doing a good job; however, some of the men have a real problem with your being a woman.'' I smiled and replied, ''You're absolutely right, Ken. They have a real problem!''

Closely related to this, the woman in the pulpit must learn to distinguish the boundaries between feedback she receives and her own opinion of her work. Younger women entering ministry often have trouble with this. Few seminarians I interviewed made any distinction between others' estimation of their preaching or administrative skills and their own, except, occasionally, to be harder on themselves than their critics. This can be a dangerous liability, especially if the criticism is misogynic.

A second strategy to help a woman preacher develop administrative leadership skills is to become more active in larger denominational conferences, seminars, and committees. She will learn from seeing how boards and agencies function in the larger institution. In addition, working side by side with judicatory leaders will help demythologize traditional power structures, enabling her to see high-ranking authorities as fallible fellow-pilgrims, in need of divine wisdom and grace just as she is. In the long run, the positive public relations of her service to the judicatory will also benefit her in other ways.

For clergywomen serving independent, nonconnectional churches, starting or joining a peer support group can aid in understanding and using ministerial authority. Ideally, each member of the group takes a turn presenting case studies concerning an event in her congregation and her role in it. Consulting with clergy peers provides reflection and feedback that the best-intentioned laity in her congregation cannot offer, because of conflicting roles and needs operating with the latter. The insights provided by other clergy not in competition with her can help the woman preacher become more intentional and consistent in liturgical and parochial leadership. Intercessory prayer support and the realization that others struggle with the same constellation of issues may also free her from the tyranny of the ''superwoman syndrome.''

Greater knowledge of the differences between the ways men and women approach decision making will equip the woman preacher to exercise more effective administrative leadership in her church. A Lutheran laywoman made the following observation about gender and the negotiating process:

Women are not heard by men. The two sexes have different viewpoints, different sets of presuppositions. The game of win-lose is more a male game than a female one. If men are not one-up, they consider themselves one-down. Women do not tend to see relationships and situations that way. Women notice the complexities of a situation; they also don't distance themselves from relationships like men do . . . and, since winning is not everything for women, the need for them to "save face" is not so compelling.[17]

Members of the church board do not need to spend time arguing whether these differences are innate, culturally conditioned, or have another source. Their more pressing need is for a pastor (male *or* female) who can recognize and work with the differences. The female pastor can serve as advocate and model for those whose voices are routinely not heard in meetings. She can help the congregation address issues in a way that is neither stereotypically masculine or feminine. One clergywoman told me about a conflict over ushers shortly after she was appointed to a church. Laity on one side claimed, "Only men can do that job." Another faction asserted, "They're only saying that because John (the head usher) doesn't like Lois" (who wanted to usher). Rather than exercising authority by making a win-lose pronouncement, or focusing on the alleged John-Lois animosity, the pastor led them into a discussion of an usher's work, and whether it made sense for the congregation to continue using only men for the job. This provided an opening for ongoing discussions of the role of laity in worship.

This clergywoman's more egalitarian style of leadership was not overruled or devalued by one group's desire for a rule to be invoked and a winner pronounced. Nor did the pastor let innuendo and interpersonal issues siphon attention from larger questions at stake. By realizing that all persons and groups do not go about decision making in the same way, she was able to claim the integrity of her own leadership style while acknowledging differing agendas. The outcome of the "usher question" did not please everyone at the meeting, but needs reflected by both groups were met; those needing measurable, tangible results had a new policy for recruiting ushers. Those whose focus was more on process and relationships had the promise of continued, open-ended discussion.

Another strategy for the woman preacher is to safeguard her self-confidence and credibility by resisting the temptations of token authority. By this I mean that for all affirmative action may do for women, it does them no favors if it accelerates them into positions for which they have inadequate training and experience. The thrill of rapid promotion to high-visibility and status appointments is quickly extinguished by anxious confusion over what the job actually requires. Furthermore, sometimes precipitous promotion in the name of affirmative action is a set-up by those who hope the woman will flounder; her failure will vindicate ongoing sexism in the church and marketplace.

This is not to suggest that clergywomen steadfastly refuse to be the "first" woman to lead the congregation through a building program, head a judicatory committee, or accept a denominational position with considerable authority. These can be avenues for acquiring competence in new fields. However, the woman preacher will do well to ask whether she has opportunities to prepare sufficiently for the challenges and scrutiny the position entails. She should also determine whether she is envisioned as the first woman of many or the "only" woman in the venture. In this way, she may not only develop her own effectiveness as a leader, but also enable her sisters in ministry to cultivate their own leadership skills.

Finally, a woman preacher may gain strength and confidence by reflecting on her call, reminding herself that it has been affirmed by her denomination in the act of ordination. She has been commissioned to lead the community of faith in the day-to-day work of the church, as well as in worship of the triune God. Reinforcing the spiritual connection between chancel and vestry will enable the clergywoman to fulfill her calling in both with integrity and credibility.

A woman preacher must take special care not to perpetuate oppression by her first-person stories, the way she speaks about other women in sermon illustrations, or by her nonverbal communication.

*C*onsciously or unconsciously, the woman preacher models for the congregation what she believes to be important and unimportant in her message. Through clothing, posture, face, and gesture she discloses her understanding of being created in the image of God, female, and called to ministry.

*H*ow does a woman preacher's body communicate from the pulpit? Though the tilting head and shallow breathing mentioned earlier suggest, "It's okay; this is just your daughter speaking," more often the preacher's gestures and changes in posture communicate, "Listen to your mother!"

FOUR

SELF-DISCLOSURE IN WOMEN'S PREACHING

When my maternal grandparents celebrated their golden wedding anniversary, they were interviewed for a feature story in the local newspaper. At one point the reporter asked my grandmother, "Mrs. Creston, to what do you attribute fifty successful years of marriage?" The petite, frail, eighty-six-year-old smiled at the interviewer and replied, "Never give an inch. Show him who's boss. Fight, fight, fight!" The reporter was taken aback by the incongruity between the old woman's appearance and her words. My grandmother was well aware of the discrepancy, and enjoyed it, knowing there was nothing more at stake than a clipping for her scrapbook.

This nonhomiletical incident illustrates, I believe, issues that pertain to a woman preacher's self-disclosure: awareness of what her physical presentation communicates, accurate assessment of those listening to her, intentional choice of words, and understanding of what risks are involved in the situation. Some of these are also issues for male preachers, of course; the difference is that when a man's self-disclosure disturbs the equilibrium of communication, it is not likely to be attributed to his gender. The congregation's heightened awareness of gender when a woman preaches means that she must take into account an additional factor; she is far more likely to be perceived as a "representative" of women than male preachers are heard as representing men. The things she says about herself and other women may be taken as permission for her listeners to view women in the same way. For example, at the beginning of this book I made reference to preaching a sermon on Simeon and Anna. An older woman in the congregation identified with both the character of Anna and with me. The result was a desire to "tell her story" to others—especially to her granddaughter, whose name was Anna.

Western culture is more sensitive to gender issues than it was a generation ago. For women in the pulpit, this is a mixed blessing. On the one hand, it means that people are ready to consider how God's word speaks to their self-understanding as sexual beings, their relationships, and the life of the church. On the other hand, it means that a woman preacher must take special care not to perpetuate oppression by her first-person stories, the way she speaks about other women in sermon illustrations, or by her nonverbal communication.

A woman serving a local church will do more to change her congregation's thinking about her (and about gender issues in general) by the "incidental" self-disclosure in week-to-week expository or topical sermons than by "Women's Sunday" and/or sermons dealing specifically with women's issues. This is because congregations can anticipate the agenda on such Sundays, and line up their arguments for or against it. Just as people expect a preacher to come out against racism on Race Relations Sunday, and "respond" to the sermon before it is preached, so also they expect certain things to be said if the sermon text is about the role of women or the guest speaker/topic will deal with gender issues. What the preacher models from the pulpit every Sunday makes a more subtle, but lasting impression on listeners.

In this chapter, therefore, little reference will be made to women's sermons that are explicitly *about* women. The self-disclosure in such homilies is evident and intentional. I will present and analyze the depiction of women as it occurs in two other ways during preaching: (1) self-disclosure in illustration and autobiographical reference; and (2) self-disclosure in nonverbal communication.

SELF-DISCLOSURE IN ILLUSTRATION AND
AUTOBIOGRAPHICAL REFERENCE

Discussion of illustration and autobiographical reference should not be limited to anecdotal material that appears as a discrete unit in the sermon. Women deliberately tell stories about themselves that place them in a favorable or unfavorable light; examples of this will be given in the paragraphs that follow. But self-disclosure also occurs in less obvious ways. For example, in the chapter on theology and interpretation, it will be shown that women preachers frequently interpret a narrative text by making a personal identification with one character in it. More often than not, the character is the least powerful in the story, or the object of action rather than the initiator. The woman's identification with the relatively powerless seems to occur regardless of her position on liberation theology. Her indirect self-disclosure suggests that the woman herself experiences a sense of "being like" the powerless one(s) in the text, though there is no way to measure empirically whether this is in fact the preacher's situation in life, or whether her congregation agrees with the assessment.

As I worked with examples of explicit references to themselves or other women in women's sermons, I discerned that more often than not, material that discussed a woman's vocation or her faith commitments transcended cultural stereotypes about masculinity and femininity. Illustrations depicting women primarily in interpersonal relationships, on the other hand, often presented women in an unfavorable light, giving the congregation permission to perpetuate a restrictive or negative understanding of what it means to be female. The basis for these observations is presented in the following paragraphs, along with implications for the woman preacher making the decision as to what she should say about herself from the pulpit, how to say it, and to what end.

TRANSCENDING OR CHALLENGING STEREOTYPES

Self-disclosure and anecdotes often transcend gender stereotypes when they are about the preacher's faith identity. Rather than necessarily "baring her soul," the preacher serves as a "representative I" for the congregation (both men and women), giving voice to their own experiences or struggles. For example, the preacher is speaking *for* the congregation as well as to them in this passage:

> In my own mind I often felt that I either had to choose between being a faithful follower of Jesus Christ or being a happy, healthy person. It took years to understand differently. I had to make a mental transition from the words "goodness" and "self-denial" to the words "honesty" and "directness." . . . I am learning that to lose one's life *does* mean to save it.[1]

There is nothing in the illustration that identifies the preacher's experience as masculine or feminine; she is expressing a religious struggle that may be common to all present. In order for the autobiographical reference to speak to all her listeners as "representative I," it must assess accurately what common ground she shares with the congregation, so that the illustration is a mirror of their experience rather than merely a window into her own.[2]

Occasionally a woman preacher will begin the sermon using first-person references to spiritual identity that function as "representative I," but then she switches to autobiographical anecdotes that cannot be heard the same way. This may confuse a congregation; they thought she was speaking about *them,* but it turns out she was not. Brief excerpts from one woman's sermon demonstrate the difficulty:

> There are times when I speak to God in monologue-like fashion. When I'm feeling threatened, weak, and helpless and that there is a lot wrong with me, I make the mistake, not of speaking from weakness, but assuming [God] cannot understand, cannot care about, and [is] unable to help me in my current distress. . . . I have spent twenty years as a woman religious, and during that period of my life I prayed and continue to pray in all three manners just described. . . . I became aware that I was living my everyday life in a religious patriarchal structure, and now it began to make less

and less sense to me. At the same time, I was undergoing a long and arduous psychoanalysis.[3]

In fairness to the preacher, she never claimed to be speaking for everyone in the congregation. But because the "representative I" references came in the first paragraph of the sermon, the congregation was led to understand that the "I" included them. When the narrative that followed departed radically from common experience, it split their focus between the preacher's thesis (maturity in prayer) and the preacher's personal tribulations. First-person references to one's Christian experience can, nevertheless, transcend gender stereotypes if the woman preacher is careful not to add details that prevent worshipers from identifying with the example being presented.

In autobiographical references to vocation, the woman preacher and her congregation may not attend at a conscious level to the "representative" nature of illustrations; yet the reference functions as a vehicle for inclusive thinking on the part of the listeners. The self-disclosure often occurs as a passing personal reference in service to another idea. For example, while introducing the contrast between the Attica Federal Penitentiary and its bucolic surroundings, one woman in the pulpit said:

In the rural upstate New York District where I serve among 52 churches, we have a lot more apple orchards and corn fields than we have subdivisions. We do live eight hours from New York City, but there is a startling statistic among those apple orchards . . . for in those five rural counties are housed over 6,000 inmates in five correctional facilities. And part of our connectional United Methodist and ecumenical ministry is the Attica Visitor Center, Attica being one of our prisons.[4]

In just a few sentences, the visiting preacher transcended gender stereotypes by showing listeners a world in which women as well as men serve churches and supervise pastors, where they know prison statistics and organize ministries based on that knowledge. In a similar vein, a woman student preaching on the parable of the wedding feast (Matthew 22:1-14) began humorously with a

67

general discussion of invitations one dare not ignore, such as the invitation she'd received that week to undergo pre-ordination psychological testing. During discussion after she preached, she said her purpose in using that example was to remind listeners of some common ground (invitation to required testing) before explicating the parable's invitation in depth. The autobiographical reference was also an (unplanned) reminder that all candidates go through the same testing, regardless of sex.

The incidence of "liberating" *first-person* references to faith-identity or vocation seem more prevalent when the woman preacher is speaking *ad clerum*—in the seminary classroom or to clergy convocations—than in the local church setting. The woman preacher may experience a greater freedom to identify herself with her work when she does not anticipate resistance to her vocation. This "assumption of support" is manifested in a sermon Christine Smith preached at a continuing education event for clergy:

> . . . Three years ago when I was in Nairobi for the United Nations' Decade For Women Conference, a group of us visited a village several hours away. We had the opportunity to witness a nutrition project, a water project, and an agricultural project begun by Catholic Relief Services.[5]

This excerpt is a telling one: the context did not require the preacher to explain (or defend) the United Nations or the idea of a Decade for Women. The speaker's presence in Nairobi was not the focus of the illustration; what happened at one of these projects was.

Illustrations and passing references to *other* women's vocations and faith commitments also seem to transcend or challenge stereotypes. Unlike the *self*-disclosing story of this type, the preacher appears to be comfortable using anecdotes about other women in sermons preached in local churches as well as to clergy gatherings. For example, a woman student preaching a Lenten sermon on John 2:13-22 began this way:

> *"Vacare deo"*—the little sign hung above writer Gertrude Mueller Nelson's sink every Lenten season.

"Vacare deo," it said: empty yourself to God. A small reminder, perhaps, but one filled with significance.[6]

The preacher's central idea was that we ought to be open, empty, and waiting for God to enter in and renew our lives. In the process of making that point, however, she depicted a world in which women write, know Latin, observe the Christian year—and also do familiar household chores. In a similar manner, a woman preaching on II Corinthians 6:14–7:1 began by telling a story about another woman using terms that challenged stereotypes:

> Several years ago a historian named Barbara Tuchman wrote a book about life in fourteenth-century Europe called *A Distant Mirror*. She gave that title to her book because the fourteenth century with its many wars, killings, diseases, shifting political allegiances, and people who sought security in weapons and kingdoms instead of God, reminded her of the twentieth century.[7]

Although both sermon introductions presented glimpses of women in terms of their vocation or faith identity, I believe the first one would "work" better in a local church. The reasons are that the preacher addressed the congregation directly, identifying herself with them; she explained the unfamiliar Latin term quickly; and there was a balance of familiarity and novelty in the anecdote. In addition to this, her relatively short sentences were easier on the ear. These are not major issues in themselves, but attending to them as she shapes communication will facilitate congregational readiness to consider new ways of thinking about the role of women in church and society.

Balancing the familiar with the novel and engaging the congregation directly are more crucial when the illustration appears at the beginning of the sermon. Later on in her message, when the preacher has established the context of her ideas, the congregation has a frame of reference for processing information otherwise quite outside their experience. For example, a woman preaching on Ruth 1:1-19 and Matthew 22:15-22 had already spoken about the extraordinary courage of ordinary women when she used this illustration:

69

These women [in Argentina] watched their daughters, sons, husbands disappear without a trace. . . . So they organized other women. . . . Wearing white kerchiefs in mourning and pictures of the lost one in their families around their necks, on a Thursday afternoon at five o'clock, fifteen women walked a silent hour vigil around the Plaza de Mayo in front of government buildings. . . . Many believe the Mothers of the Plaza de Mayo . . . helped bring the downfall of that government and the return of democracy to Argentina.[8]

It should be noted that the "strangeness" of foreign women being political activists is balanced by the familiarity of women depicted as wives and mothers. The congregation has two ways of making the connection between the Mothers of the Plaza de Mayo and their own world; they can use the frame of reference ("ordinary women") already given to them by the preacher, or they can resonate with the familiar depiction of women as wives and mothers. This illustration is distinctive in the way that it presents women as simultaneously powerless and powerful. They are powerless to protect their families, but powerful as a group in protesting against an unjust government. Stereotypes are both affirmed and challenged. Unlike the other examples cited, this illustration was from a sermon primarily about women, and the changes they can make when committed to a cause. In women's preaching, nonstereotypical illustrations about women in relationship to others are most likely to occur when the message itself is about women.

REINFORCING STEREOTYPES

When a woman preacher's self-disclosure or illustration about other women depicts women in relationship to others, gender stereotypes are reinforced more often than not. This seems to occur regardless of the theological or political viewpoint of the preacher, or the context in which the sermon is preached. One may argue that "traditional" relationships are not in themselves necessarily oppressive; however, much of the material available unwittingly presents these relationships in a way that is unfavorable to women.

How does this happen? One way it occurs is when a relational illustration is perceived not as explicating a specific idea in the sermon, or explaining how the preacher came to hold a particular point of view, but rather as an attempt to cultivate intimacy or mutual vulnerability with the congregation. The stereotype being reinforced in such self-disclosure is that in relationships, women always want more. They're pushing for greater emotional intimacy than the other party is ready to give. For example, a woman student, preaching about God's grace extended to us when we are unlovable, told the congregation the following:

> You don't appreciate such love until you realize how undeserved it is. I remember one day recently when I was in a rotten mood. Just a bunch of little things had gone wrong: nothing major. But it piled up and piled up, and when my husband came home I started in griping at him. He'd had a rough day, too, but instead of arguing or trying to top my tale of woe, he put his arms around me and told me he loved me.

Any illustration about unmerited love will necessarily be relational. In the above example, however, the preacher has gone "too far" in revealing something about a second party and inviting congregational voyeurism. She has also used cliches that minimize the seriousness with which listeners are to take her distress, and implicitly asked them to figure out why she was out of sorts and to love her anyway. The self-disclosure diverts listeners' attention from the topic of divine grace to speculation about premenstrual syndrome and confirmation that women are indeed cranky and demanding.

A second example of a relational illustration fostering an uncomfortable or contrived closeness was given by a guest preacher who did not know her congregation. She read long excerpts from the diary kept during her last pregnancy, as a way of introducing the idea that many ministers may feel they do not have much to offer a needy world. Her awareness of the intrusive or demanding nature of such intimate details was manifested elsewhere in the sermon:

71

> June, 1980: went to another church meeting, they asked me how I was feeling, I said, I threw up eight times today, once in the shower. People looked at me rather funny, someone said, "The first item on the agenda tonight is . . ." I have no idea what it was, for I was too embarrassed about being an unseemly part of the Body of Christ.[9]

Emotional exhibitionism or the demand for greater intimacy than listeners are ready for is one way that women's self-disclosure reinforces negative stereotypes. Another common way in which personal stories work against a woman preacher's credibility is when her relational anecdotes suggest ambivalence about her priorities and/or call to preach. Consider this example, from an Advent sermon based on Luke 21:25-36:

> As [my 100-year-old grandmother] recalls things in her memory, she is able to put the right people in the right place, but her timing is not totally accurate. . . . Granny reminded me that I am 36 years old and still have no husband. She told me I had better get busy and find a man to take care of me. . . . She knew that I am a minister. She thinks it is wonderful that her granddaughter is a preacher. She had these things in the right context, but when I got ready to leave her, she told me to be careful on my way home because the old horse I was riding might give me some trouble.[10]

In this self-disclosing narrative, listeners heard not only the preacher's ambivalence about the direction of her life, but also reinforcement of stereotypes about the aged. Another woman, preaching to a seminary congregation on Acts 1, focused on Christ's promise of the Holy Spirit, and how the disciples waited for fulfillment of that promise. To illustrate their anticipation, she described the thrill of getting a letter from her boyfriend during her first miserable semester at divinity school. She clasped her hands over her bosom, then caressed her own cheeks as she told listeners about the agony of waiting, and the promise of fulfillment when the boyfriend sent her a picture of an engagement ring. Love stories do not have to present women in an unfavorable light (though I have reservations about their appropriateness in the context of worship). This preacher's body language, combined with the way this story was told and the lack of other examples, created the impression that engagement was all she knew or cared about concerning promise and fulfillment.

Sometimes women's autobiographical references are not obviously relational, but nevertheless encourage the congregation to think of her in terms of feminine stereotypes. One student began a sermon on discipleship by quoting a nursery rhyme:

> There was a crooked man who walked a crooked mile;
> He found a crooked sixpence upon a crooked stile.
> He bought a crooked cat that caught a crooked mouse,
> and they all lived together in a crooked little house.

Several people in the class reacted negatively to this, saying that by her recitation of a nursery rhyme from memory, the woman preacher adopted a mother-toddler relationship with the congregation, and/or suggested that familiarity with nursery rhymes was a woman's proper field of expertise. Where a man beginning his sermon in the same way might be perceived as challenging sex-role stereotypes, a woman reciting the poem reinforced these prejudices.

A final example of first-person narrative perpetuating stereotypes is found in a sermon from the *Women of the Word* anthology. The preacher's stated purpose was to invite the congregation to consider the way Amos spoke about a physical law to describe God's response to Israel:

> Of all things that seem unlike me, I have been reading a physics book. . . . My science background is very limited. I don't think of myself as someone who knows or is interested in science, physics, or complicated things like that. . . . Also, this week, I have been moving. . . . It seemed to me that the more I threw out the more there was to throw out. I'll admit I'm not a good housekeeper, but I don't know where most of that clutter came from. Then there is the question of dust. . . ."[11]

The preacher spoke from the world in which she and her congregation live (as opposed to the "imaginary" world of canned

73

sermon illustrations, used by men far more than women). Unfortunately, nearly everything she disclosed about herself could be used to suggest she should stick to housework and leave preaching, physics, and "complicated things like that" to competent males.

Most troubling is women's tendency to let relational anecdotes reinforce negative stereotypes about other women. As noted earlier, sermons on "women's topics" or texts, or sermons preached to gatherings of women only do not manifest this tendency. Yet it is disturbing to consider the lack of awareness and self-esteem that gives voice to illustrations that trivialize or denigrate women in other situations.

A seemingly innocent example was given by a woman preaching on John 4:5-26. She described the woman at the well as resisting an encounter with the person Jesus really was. Jesus was talking to her on the level of identity and relationship, but she tried to evade his questions. The preacher's contemporary analogies were: (1) her counselor understanding her better than she did herself; (2) a conversation between a man and a woman, in which the man was more candid; (3) an argument between her daughter and another seven-year-old girl over whether to play with Barbie dolls or a Smurf game.[12] In the first two examples, women needed to "get their act together" and were portrayed less favorably than men. In the third illustration, mention of Barbies and Smurfs discourages the congregation from taking the relationship between the girls very seriously. The preacher wrote well, and may have assessed her listeners accurately, but she seemed unaware of the way three relational stories about women being used to illustrate a text involving a woman would give a strong "representative" message: that this is the way women are.

It may be that preaching women get so caught up in the main idea being communicated that they lose sight of the messages being given in relational stories involving women. Because women in general use fewer generic illustrations and more stories from their own experience, this preacher might have been reluctant to alter details to make the cumulative effect of these anecdotes a less negative view of women. In a sermon expounding the idea that submitting to the will of God will mean an end to injustice and oppression, a preacher began with these two illustrations:

> I recall an elderly woman approaching me on her cane. She was shaking with anger. . . . She said, "If this decision is made I will see to it that the church does not receive the money my husband left in his will." Her body language as well as her words showed that SHE WAS INDEED a "Pillar of the Church!" . . . I remembered the words spoken by a Caucasian friend of mine as the two of us shared a cup of coffee and discussed the racial tension within ours and other denominations, and in society in general. "But, Teenie," she had exclaimed, "you can't mean that you think our churches ought to be integrated. That's all we've got left!"[13]

Other than brief mention of a teenage girl on a UNICEF poster, the preacher offered no other images of women in the sermon. There were no contemporary anecdotes about men. The lasting impression left by her recollection of these conversations was that women are bigots, because that was the only way they were characterized in the sermon.

The underlying negativity in the aforementioned sermon can go a step further, if the woman preacher positively reinforces prejudicial attitudes and actions towards them. For example, when preaching to a clergy convention about overcoming temptation, a woman presented a story of a man who told his wife she must not spend so much of his paycheck on clothes. He advised her, "when you go into the store and see something we can't afford, just say, 'get behind me, Satan!' " A few days later, while shopping, the woman decided it wouldn't hurt just to try on a dress that caught her eye. Tempted to buy it as she saw her reflection in the mirror, she exclaimed, "Get behind me, Satan!" (The preacher then mimicked the body language of a man appraising a woman.) The woman heard a voice behind her say, "Yea, it looks pretty good from back here, too!"[14] The congregation laughed in appreciation, and the preacher was unaware that she had given consent to the idea of males controlling money and females. She affirmed a

75

world hostile to all women (including herself), seeing women as morally weak and valued only for their sexual attractiveness.

IMPLICATIONS FOR ILLUSTRATIONS
AND AUTOBIOGRAPHICAL REFERENCES

Illustrations like the one just noted clearly damage the credibility of women preachers. In the case of this sermon, the appearance and bearing of a woman telling the story offset, to some degree, the negative stereotype reinforced by her words. By what guidelines may the woman (or man) in the pulpit make responsible decisions about self-disclosure and references to other women? A first step is examining manuscripts of her last five sermons; the preacher should ask herself what she has told the congregation about her own life in those messages. What passing remarks gave listeners a view of her life outside the pulpit, and is it the picture she wants to present? Does her self-disclosure focus on her vocation, her faith commitments, her relationships, or something else? Is a particular personal reference in service to her message, or is it only an expression of her own needs for vulnerability and intimacy? The preacher should also consider her illustrations involving other people, asking to what extent they reinforce positive or negative stereotypes, or acknowledge the existence of some people while ignoring others.

Additional factors to be taken into account when considering self-disclosure and references are: (1) assessing the congregation—what balance of familiar and novel images will "work" in a particular context? What is her tradition's understanding of the nature of Christian worship that may make an illustration fitting in one place but unsuitable in others? (2) understanding what is at stake in the use of personal references—for example, any reference to one's love life is not worth the high likelihood that the congregation's train of thought will derail and spend the remainder of the sermon speculating on the details the preacher did *not* share; (3) acknowledging the "representative bias" operating when a woman preaches, and being doubly careful about saying things that will be taken as true about all women; (4) adhering to theological convictions—if the preacher believes that all people are precious in God's sight, she will avoid illustrations that suggest there are exceptions to this tenet; and (5) awareness of the varieties of nonverbal communication that may underscore or undermine what she is saying. This issue is addressed in the section that follows.

SELF-DISCLOSURE IN NONVERBAL COMMUNICATION

This is more than a matter of commenting on what is aesthetically pleasing or conventional. Nonverbal communication is a theological issue; the preacher reinforces or negates spoken sermon content by it. Consciously or unconsciously, the woman preacher models for the congregation what she believes to be important and unimportant in her message. Through clothing, posture, face, and gesture she discloses her understanding of being created in the image of God, female, and called to ministry. Nonverbal communication, like the first-person reference or story about other women, is linked to gender expectations in our culture. One writer describes how gestures are perceived as gender-related:

> Gender gestures constitute messages about self, other, and situation simultaneously. They convey the social definitions of gender to people in particular situations. . . . Gender display may be the direct result of sex-role identification rather than sex per se.[15]

Nonverbal communication shapes listener perception more than people recognize; some believe up to 90 percent of a speaker's influence depends on it.[16] In addition to this, the English language has a redundancy rate of around 50 percent. Therefore, attending to nonverbal communication yields a more accurate assessment of what occurs when women preach than studying sermon manuscripts alone. In this section, nonverbal self-disclosure is discussed under three headings: attire (including "props" used in the pulpit), the face and head, and body language/gestures.

Some observations about women's nonverbal communication may strike the reader as overcritical. Negativity is not intended,

77

nor is the impression that the characteristics being noted are the *only* nonverbal communication used by women in the pulpit. The most noticeable and distinguishing body language—in women or men—is apt to be self-disclosure that "interrupts" the spoken message, because it draws attention to itself in ways nonverbal communication that is congruent with the spoken word does not.

SELF-DISCLOSURE IN ATTIRE

Wearing special clothes to mark particular occasions or functions is so universal a phenomenon in human history that it may be regarded as a natural cultural law.[17] The first documented use of clothing worn specifically for liturgical use may be traced back to the fourth century. The special clothing worn for leading worship and especially celebrating the Eucharist was clothing for men, though it was, by modern standards, "feminine" with its long, flowing dress. When women began to be ordained in traditions that used liturgical vestments, they and the churches faced the question of what these new clergy should wear. Should they adopt what had been exclusively menswear, or modify that clothing to fit a woman's body? Should they design a new line of liturgical vestments invested with new symbolism, or preach and celebrate in mufti?

In most mainline Protestant denominations in the United States, women preachers have had considerable latitude in deciding what to wear in the pulpit. Congregations do not have enough experience of different women leading worship to expect a certain kind of attire. Each clothing option mentioned above communicates a different nonverbal message to which theological interpretation may be made. What is distinctive about women's nonverbal communication in attire is not uniformity in appearance or rationale for the way they present themselves; it is rather the common gender-related concern that affects their decision making. Contemporary male clergy do not have to worry about acceptance or nonacceptance by the church on the basis of gender, and therefore do not have to think in terms of vestments that will play down or celebrate their sexuality.

A woman in one of my preaching classes several years ago was characteristic of one type of self-disclosure through dress. She was meticulously groomed in a ruffled pink blouse and matching skirt, and wore tasteful gold jewelry. Her hair, makeup, and nails appeared to have been done at a beauty salon. As she preached, one hand draped gracefully over the edge of the pulpit, offering people in front pews opportunity to inspect her manicure. During discussion afterward, when she was asked about her appearance, she explained that feeling pretty bolstered her self-confidence. She didn't really feel like a minister yet, but had received compliments about her clothing at her field education church. The color pink and an abundance of ruffles, in our culture, communicate femininity, sexual immaturity, sentimentality, and fragility.[18]

Another woman in the class said she, too, wore "nice clothes" rather than a robe while preaching. Her reason was that a robe set her apart from the laity, while dressing like any other woman in the congregation made her feel like one of them. Though both students were competent sermon-writers, the nonverbal self-disclosure their congregations probably "heard" was that they were sweet (and powerless) girls who weren't going to upset anybody in the church by what they said or did. After graduating from seminary and being called to a pastorate, one reported difficulty in being taken seriously by her congregation. This problem may have been due to her nonverbal communication conflicting with the prophetic words she spoke from the pulpit. In his essay, "We Had to Sacrifice the Woman," Thomas Troeger mentioned the frustration and even rage people in a homiletics class experienced when a woman preacher used pink yarn—suggesting childlike helplessness and/or femininity in our culture—as a symbol to address a difficult social issue.[19]

An increasing number of women are purchasing or designing liturgical vestments made for women. These range from familiar garments tailored especially for women and/or stoles with more "feminine" religious symbols, to liturgical clothing and symbols few laypeople can identify. In group photographs of newly-ordained clergy in The United Methodist Church, for instance, one will see far more variety in the liturgical attire of the women than of the men. The nonverbal communication in these specially made albs, Geneva gowns, and stoles is not likely to alienate or confuse most congregations. The clothing and symbols are close enough to what people have experienced before to suggest continuity with established patterns of worship.

At the same time, the women's clothing acknowledges that the communication event is not exactly the same as what worshipers have known in the past. Bizarre symbols, shapes, and colors are more apt to divert attention from the spoken word than colors and shapes that are subconsciously already understood as part of the communication event. Contrast the women's cassocks sold in the Almy or Cokesbury catalogs with the dramatically different attire for women in worship prescribed by Rosemary Radford Ruether's "rite of healing from rape" in *Women-Church*. The chief person in the liturgy is "clothed in a festive dress with a crown of sage leaves and a bouquet of flowers and herbs."[20] In fairness to Ruether's rite, the chief person is not proclaiming the Word or officiating as in a regular Sunday morning service. However, the liturgy itself contains no explanation of why the woman puts on these articles; the meaning is unclear. When the woman preacher's clothing is altogether foreign to the worship experience of the congregation, the "noise" or dissonance created by anxiety over what it signifies drowns out whatever words she speaks. Worshipers are likely to see the difference as gender-related (having been given no other way to account for it), and feel first threatened and then defensive or angry about the ambiguity.

A third option for women preachers' self-disclosure through dress is simply using the liturgical vestments traditionally worn by clergymen. When Barbara Harris was consecrated the first woman bishop in the Episcopal Church in 1989, the photographs printed by newspapers and magazines around the world invariably depicted her wearing chasuble and mitre, and carrying a crozier. The clothing in this case made a powerful symbolic statement as a badge of office. It was nonverbal communication that delighted some and infuriated others before she said a word. By wearing a "sacred" uniform formerly restricted to men, she challenged the validity of the restrictions; conservative Episcopalians might say

SELF-DISCLOSURE IN WOMEN'S PREACHING

she challenged the sacredness of the office. There is also the objection on the part of women that to adopt clothing formerly worn only by men is to accommodate a male-dominated, hierarchical ecclesiology she does not want to communicate to the congregation. To quote one woman preacher:

> What do I wear to preach? That depends on the liturgical season, the weather, and my mood. Mostly my mood. I don't want to look like a man in the pulpit. I don't want the congregation to say, "see, it's really no different from having a man up there."[21]

What does all this mean for the woman seminarian about to pastor her first church? First, she should not assume that a particular vestment is appropriate simply because it is featured in a religious supply-house catalog. She may go through such a catalog with laypeople and discuss the theological and ecclesiological assumptions being communicated in each model. There may be a remarkable number of interpretations of what different vestments and colors mean. Next, the woman may ask herself what factors already influence her inclination to wear one thing or another while leading worship. How accountable is she to a given liturgical tradition? What kind of vestments were worn by the last pastor? She may also investigate what opportunities there are in the church program for "decoding" the nonverbal communication of an unfamiliar vestment. In this way, the woman minister and her congregation can name and deal with visual impediments to effective communication in the pulpit.

SELF-DISCLOSURE THROUGH HEAD AND FACIAL EXPRESSION

Among nonverbal communications with face and head that appear to be gender-related in our culture are the position and mobility of the head while speaking, duration of gaze and smiles during conversation, intuitive responsiveness to the nonverbal communication of others, and intonation.[22] Men and women differ in the ways these are employed, and although people in the pews

81

don't consciously keep track of how they occur, they do affect the way listeners perceive the preacher.

One communications expert identified turning the head upward or tilting it to the side as feminine nonverbal communication used in interaction with males.[23] It is also associated with dependency, coyness, and the need for adult approval. Evie Tornquist-Karlsson, a contemporary Christian musician, released a song several years ago that mentions another bit of body language involving the head:

> Whenever they say, "How can you preach to people who reach down and pat you on the head?" "Well," I say, "we should all be like children reaching up to Him instead."[24]

The reference to children is a telling one; when a woman in the pulpit engages in tilting or bobbing of the head, it usually does not come across as deliberate or adult sexual manipulation. The preacher interacts with grown-up listeners as a daughter rather than as a sweetheart or peer. The tilt of the head suggests diffidence rather than overt flirtatiousness. It is frequently accompanied by more shallow breathing, scissors-crossing of the legs (a truly self-protective gesture) and a rising inflection at the end of sentences (for example, "let us pray?").[25]

Younger women in the pulpit manifest these patterns of head movement more than older ones. In preaching classes, I have observed that this nonverbal communication most often occurs: (1) at the beginning of the sermon, and (2) when something challenging, prophetic, or otherwise "difficult" is being said. One woman, speaking on the necessity of working out one's own salvation, tossed her curls, tilted her head, and began to lisp as she spoke about a military truck on a suicide mission. The body language was so incongruous with the sermon content it led me to believe that the nonverbal communication was asking permission to say uncomfortable words to the congregation. The head movements revealed the young woman's need to placate listeners and sustain the equilibrium of the relationship.

A congregation may "hear" this self-disclosing communication in various ways. It may be received unconsciously to offset hard words being spoken, and thus function effectively. It may also be interpreted as the preacher calling them to interact at a deeper level of intimacy (that of a parent-daughter relationship) than they are willing to do. In the latter case, the wobbling head will evoke resistance and perhaps impatience with what is perceived as inappropriate cuteness.

A sustained gaze and intuitive responsiveness to listeners, identified by communications experts as characteristic feminine interaction patterns, are also typical of women's self-disclosure in the pulpit. This nonverbal interaction usually functions as an asset in preaching, unless the gaze is so prolonged it is perceived as a challenging stare. Not surprisingly, the gaze is most likely to be sustained when the preacher reiterates something she has already said, when she tells a story, or when she says something she considers is of crucial importance. Male students, by contrast, will use briefer eye contact but "freeze" a gesture and speak with different diaphragmatic support for emphasis. The woman's self-disclosing metacommunication at such moments is, "I'm speaking to your heart from my own. Do you understand what I mean?" A listener in the pews is apt to feel personally addressed by this nonverbal message; the person's understanding and response matter to this preacher.

Duration of smiles, also noted by experts as gender-related nonverbal communication, is not a significant factor in women preachers. The problem of coming across as overly solemn or manic afflicts both men and women, but not with notable frequency. It may be that smiles of longer duration are more typical of women in one-on-one conversation or small group dialogue than in preaching.

SELF-DISCLOSURE IN BODY LANGUAGE AND GESTURE

Only a few women whose preaching I have witnessed over the years stood like robots in the pulpit, disclosing nothing of themselves in gesture or a shift in posture. There is a fair degree of consistency in the types of gestures and postures women preachers

83

employ, and those suggest an overlap of women's roles in the pulpit with other spheres of activity, particularly mothering. In *Weaving the Sermon,* Smith champions a body-oriented feminist spirituality:

> The church's oppressive attitudes and moralizing regarding sexuality at all levels of human existence have emerged in part from a total denial of the body. Misogyny and homophobia have also been fueled by a denial of our bodies and a denial of sexual/sensual/relational expression.[26]

How does a woman preacher's body communicate from the pulpit? Though the tilting head and shallow breathing mentioned earlier suggest, "It's okay; this is just your daughter speaking," more often the preacher's gestures and changes in posture communicate, "Listen to your mother!" The preacher discloses this by a sequence of gestures at key moments in the sermon. While a younger woman preacher may bob her head, and a man is likely to fumble with the coins in his pocket to relieve tension, during prophetic utterance a remarkable number of women make short, stroking gestures at elbow height, close to the body, and rock slightly from side to side. It is the same body language used by a mother to comfort a fretful infant or small child. The movement of the arm from the elbow down is consistent with one author's observation that in a man's presence, a woman pulls her body in, to take up less space.[27] The preacher's hand, however, is extended and makes repeated gestures with no closure.

The "mother" body language may be communicated in other ways, some of which may be perceived as menacing by the congregation. A woman who was class president preached in the seminary chapel, using Matthew 5 as her text. When she reached the point in her sermon where she discussed "being persecuted for righteousness' sake," one hand went up on her hip and stayed there for several minutes. The other hand was often extended from the elbow, waving palm up and slightly to one side. After the service I overheard two men making angry comments about the preacher, but their criticism was not specifically about sermon content. I believe the preacher's body language said, "I know what I'm talking about, and you'd better listen!"

Some scholars believe a woman in a position of authority awakens listeners' preverbal relationship with their mother. When her voice and body language challenge rather than soothe, listeners feel like scolded, rebellious children.[28] Another woman preacher used maternal body language as she made an analogy between a child's need for discipline and a Christian's need to submit to God's will. She described a mother who, finding her baby would not settle down in its crib, gently but firmly pressed down on the child's back so it could not fidget anymore. The preacher emphasized this by pressing her right hand flat upon the pulpit; unfortunately, she let it remain in that position several minutes as she continued speaking in a calm, deliberate manner. It was difficult for me to concentrate on her words, because her body language had me "pinned down" on her previous idea. It was threatening, though that was not her intent.

The inflection of a woman preacher's voice, along with head and body language, combine to suggest a quality or degree of relationship between preacher and listeners that is different from what the congregation experiences with male preachers. In emphasizing the truthfulness of a point, for example, a woman in the pulpit often draws her hands together over her bosom. A man is more likely to raise his right hand as though swearing on a Bible, or point upwards. In the United States, there is little crossover in these gestures, though both sexes share other body language for emphasizing the integrity of a statement.[29]

The woman's body language, it should be noted, draws the listener into greater intimacy than the man's. If we exaggerate the possible differences in nonverbal self-disclosure, it is not difficult to understand why congregations "hear" men and women differently. Her voice often rises at the end of a sentence, as though asking for congregational assent. His inflection drops, as though making a pronouncement or giving an order. Her eye contact is more sustained and "personal" than his. Her gestures suggest familial relationships; his maintain distance and remind listeners of the courtroom. The masculine nonverbal interaction tells worshipers that obedience and respect are expected. They are not asked for the same physical, emotional, and spiritual involvement as the feminine nonverbal communication.

IMPLICATIONS FOR WOMEN'S NONVERBAL SELF-DISCLOSURE

Masculine body language is not better than feminine in the pulpit—or vice versa. A woman preacher who aims for androgynous or asexual self-disclosure in her nonverbal communication is likely to encounter just as many problems as one who is stereotypically feminine. A better goal for women (and men) in the pulpit is to be intentional rather than accidental about congruity between verbal and nonverbal communication. Physical presence and words spoken should focus listener attention on the gospel being proclaimed, rather than heightening awareness of the one proclaiming it. For the preacher with access to videotaping equipment, a simple exercise can help her identify body language that conflicts with her sermon. Invite someone who was not present at worship to view the videotape of the service with the volume turned off, and ask him or her to guess what was being communicated by the preacher. If the discrepancy is great, the woman preacher should then ask the viewer to identify as specifically as possible the gestures and expressions that created the misleading impression. The videotape will also point out distracting and repetitive gestures.

Even without a videocamera, the woman preacher may take several steps to enhance her nonverbal self-disclosure. First, the "head-tilting" habit can be overcome by sticking a small piece of invisible tape just below and behind the ear. It won't prevent mobility, but the slight pull every time her head starts to wobble may prompt the question, "is this the right gesture at the moment?" Second, though pre-planned gestures look inauthentic, body language resulting from reflection on sermon content does not. A preacher may go over her manuscript and outline, asking herself what she would like the congregation to perceive or experience at various points. If she can establish this in her own mind, she is more likely to embody what she is saying, and facilitate appropriate congregational response. Heightened awareness of the liturgical season or occasion in the life of the congregation also aids in nonverbal communication that is congruous with message content. A congregation does not expect the preacher to beam like a game-show host on Maundy Thursday, no matter how glad she is to be worshiping with them!

Finally, the preacher may study and describe the people who come on Sunday morning: their expectations of worship, their beliefs about masculinity and femininity in general, and the ways they communicate nonverbally. The purpose in this is not necessarily to mirror or reinforce their biases, but to be able to "read" them and interact more effectively during the act of preaching.

*F*eminist assumptions about the nature of the canon are not representative of all women who preach. The use of one of these [liberation/feminist] methodological tools, then, may or may not indicate the preacher's affinity with liberation/feminist interpretation.

*T*he male preacher is more apt to tell the congregation what they should do, rather than who they are.

*I*f the preacher uses identification with the less powerful in the text as an interpretive method, she may effectively grant permission for listeners to be similarly vulnerable. A congregation that understands itself as powerless in some way will find this method of interpretation both liberating and comforting. If the preacher consistently uses this method . . . the congregation may perceive it as begging for affirmation or lacking conviction.

*M*y conviction is that the predilection to interpret texts in terms of achieving equilibrium in relationships is not a conscious decision made by women preachers, but reflects Gilligan's and Eriksson's assertion that feminine identity is awakened or established in a relationship of intimacy with another person.

FIVE

WOMEN PREACHERS AND BIBLICAL INTERPRETATION

What method of biblical interpretation, if any, can be called "typical" for women? Do exegetical insights appear in women's sermons in a predictable pattern? Though any answers to these questions may be rejected as sexist and stereotypical, they are questions that interest feminist and nonfeminist homileticians. No consensus presently exists among seminary homileticians concerning the differences in preaching among their male and female students.[1] As one feminist scholar analyzed sermons by women, she discerned that feminist women preachers regularly used a feminist or liberation hermeneutic for interpretation of the biblical text. The feminist hermeneutic often included modifying language about God in text and sermon to make it gender-inclusive or mutual.[2]

But *feminist* is an elusive term; it means different things to different people. Some homileticians maintain that any woman preacher communicates a kind of feminism, because her very presence in the pulpit challenges patriarchal stereotypes.[3] This is in contrast to the point of view that both men and women may be feminists, but it is a self-conscious, not incidental approach to homiletics or any other endeavor.[4]

Still another school of thought would divide feminist interpreters of the Bible into three groups: (1) biblical feminists, who see Scripture as the primary source of theology and a central authority that cannot be evaded; (2) liberation feminists, who embrace the methodology developed by liberation theology, but whose primary interest is the liberation of women; and (3) radical feminists, or rejectionists, who view both Scripture and tradition as irredeemably oppressive, and who disengage women's struggle toward liberation from a presumed "general" human liberation.[5] The greatest number of women who identify themselves as feminists would likely be found in the second group. These are interpreters who approach texts and commentaries with a "hermeneutic of suspicion." This language, borrowed from liberation theology, means that the interpreter is always prepared to ask whether the biblical text was recorded from the perspective of the powerful, and to what extent prevailing interpretations of the passage found in commentaries reflect a cultural agenda or bias. Feminist biblical scholars, such as Elisabeth Schüssler Fiorenza, identify this bias as patriarchy:

> A feminist hermeneutics cannot trust or accept Bible and tradition simply as divine revelation. Rather it must critically evaluate them as patriarchal articulations . . . feminist hermeneutics has ramifications not only for historical scholarship but also for our contemporary political situation because the Bible still functions today as a religious justification and ideological legitimization of patriarchy.[6]

Another feminist scholar, Phyllis Trible, recognizes the patriarchal confines of the Bible as ancient document and the varied meanings of a text, but she uses rhetorical criticism to discover "subversive" exegetical insights. Her "eschatological vision" is that people move toward a theology of gender redemption, returning to a creation in the image of God.[7]

That feminist preachers would employ a feminist hermeneutic in sermon preparation is self-evident. Ambiguity enters the picture when one stops speaking about feminist interpretation, which most homileticians use to designate a chosen hermeneutical perspective, and begins to speak of *women's* interpretation of a text for preaching. It may be true that the mere presence of a woman in the pulpit challenges old stereotypes (feminist by default), but that does not speak to the issue of interpretation per se. In this chapter, excerpts from sermons will be used to demonstrate three points: first, women's sermons regularly manifest several features in exegetical method that concur with liberation and/or feminist hermeneutics as set forth by Justo and Catherine Gonzalez and Elisabeth Schüssler Fiorenza. Second, these similarities do not necessarily indicate a feminist perspective on the part of the woman preacher. Finally, there are additional characteristic features in women's exposition of texts that appear to be gender-related in terms of women's psychological development.

WOMEN AS FEMINIST/LIBERATION EXEGETES

1. "Same Text, Different Story"

An interpretive method often manifested in sermons by women is that of presenting a familiar text but emphasizing aspects of it that were previously unnoticed or deemed unimportant. In setting aside prevailing and "safe" approaches to a pericope, new perspectives may offer fresh and perhaps radical insights. A hermeneutic of suspicion brought to bear on well-worn material demonstrates how some voices routinely have not been heard, either in the original context or the preacher's own. An example of this is found in Nancy Hastings Sehested's sermon in *And Blessed Is She*. Even the title, "Let Pharaoh Go" (based on Exodus 1:8-22) indicates that the story will be told from a previously unexamined perspective. She writes:

> Shiphrah and Puah, not exactly household names . . . ordinary women who did extraordinary things . . . they showed enormous courage—playing a large role in the redemptive history of Israel. [Pharaoh] called in the Hebrew midwives for this one: Shiphrah and Puah . . . for the good of the nation and for the security of the children of Egypt, he wanted them to be part of a secret and daring mission to kill all the boy Hebrew babies . . . But Shiphrah and Puah knew who they were. They knew they had no power before Pharaoh. So they let Pharaoh go—to think his own thoughts—to go his own way—while they followed their way assisting in life.[8]

The text for this sermon is usually remembered in terms of Israel's bondage in Egypt, why Pharaoh was considered a tyrant, and/or the background of Moses' story. "Suspicion" of the prevailing interpretations led Sehested to concentrate on two figures in the narrative whose situation spoke to the context of the congregation listening to the sermon.

How might Sehested have moved from initial curiosity about the text to the decision to focus on the action and motives of the midwives? If one assumes there is a basic affinity between feminist and other liberation theologies, the preacher may employ the "hermeneutic circle" as the starting point for interpreting a text for preaching. The movements in the circle are as follows:

> Firstly, there is our way of experiencing reality, which leads us to ideological suspicion. Secondly, there is the application of our ideological suspicion to the superstructure in general and to theology in particular. Thirdly, there comes a new way of experiencing theological reality that leads us to exegetical suspicion, that is, to the suspicion that the prevailing interpretation of the Bible has not taken important pieces of data into account. Fourth, we have our new hermeneutic, that is, our new way of interpreting the fountainhead of our faith (i.e., Scripture) with the new elements at our disposal.[9]

For the feminist, the experience of oppressive patriarchy is the reality that women bring to theology and interpretation in particular. It is the lens through which all texts are seen, but those which traditionally have been expounded with a misogynist bias are particularly under scrutiny. The interpreter investigates data that have not been taken into account, data that reveal God's liberating word in the midst of androcentric texts. In Exodus 1:8-22, patriarchy is clear; a male ruler decrees that all male Hebrew children (who pose a potential threat to his power) shall be killed. Females, by default, are so powerless there is no need to eliminate them. The liberating word in the text is that not only is the oppressor thwarted; it happens at the hands of those without power. There is solidarity between God and courageous women.

"Letting Pharaoh go" means defiantly resisting the injustice of the powerful in any time or place.

The hermeneutic of suspicion evokes fresh insights on familiar passages. But this hermeneutic can exercise its own tyranny, sometimes without the preacher's awareness. This is commonly manifested in increased focus on human power struggles and diminished proclamation about divine-human interaction. For example, in the discussion of theological and homiletical concerns following this particular sermon, Sehested recorded some of the questions that came to mind as she studied the text: What is God's word to victims of oppression? What does this story say about God's ways of empowering the weak and the powerless? But divine activity does not appear as a major issue in the sermon; God isn't even mentioned until the end of the fourth page, and functions mainly as a source of identity rather than as Shiphrah and Puah's Lord, the covenant-maker, or the initiator of liberation.

A second approach to Scripture as "same text, different story" is Phyllis Trible's use of rhetorical criticism. The rhetorical structure of a text itself in its original language (and often in the English translation) focuses the reader's attention on new issues. Though Trible's writing is not in sermon form, her insights are used widely by feminist preachers. In her exposition of the book of Ruth, the text's patriarchal bias is revealed. Once it is exposed for what it is, it loses its authority:

> Third person narration names the [female] characters, specifies their relationships, and describes their plight, but it does not allow them to emerge as human beings. Subjects of verbs, they are objects of discourse; spoken about, they do not speak. Accordingly, they hover between person and nonperson . . . [Naomi] "was bereft of her two children and her husband" (v. 5). From wife to widow, from mother to no-mother, this female is stripped of all identity.[10]

It is clear, from this excerpt of Trible's work with the text, that it will not develop into a sermon explaining the ancestry of the Messiah, or be used for a wedding homily on the virtues of fidelity.

2. "Getting Down to Cases"

A second characteristic of biblical interpretation by women preachers is use of concrete analogy between the biblical context and the contemporary one. Generic stories from books of sermon illustrations are scarce in women's preaching; instead, the tendency is to identify the action or direction of the text, and demonstrate it with immediate and/or accessible experience touching the lives of people in the congregation. Sometimes this requires what Fred Craddock calls the "direct transfer" method of interpretation, but more often the preacher does "interpretation of intent," for example, working beyond surface biases or problems in the text to discern the liberating word. In the preached sermon, the concrete analogy in contemporary context frequently gets more attention than the passage from which the analogy is drawn. An example of this may be found in Carole Carlson's sermon in *Spinning a Sacred Yarn*. Based on Deuteronomy 10:12-22 and Luke 18:9-14, the sermon "America—Finished or Unfinished," was preached the Sunday after All Souls Day and the 1980 general election:

> In thinking about today's sermon and the upcoming election, and putting that idea together with the image of all those souls in purgatory, I decided there must be some connection between the two. . . . Never in our history has there been a presidential contest where people were so uninterested, indifferent, or outright negative. Why do we feel such a sense of hopelessness about Tuesday? . . . we have reached the deplorable situation in this country where the ability to get elected has absolutely nothing to do with the ability to govern. . . . the candidates who are presented all too often seem like the Pharisees of 1980. Like today's candidates who are certain of what the people want to hear, the Pharisee knew what God wanted to hear. . . . caring for children—for all who are in need—is *God's* priority during this election week.[11]

One hazard in gleaning the concrete, political significance of the text in sermon preparation but not in proclamation is that the congregation must figure out the analogy without assistance. The hermeneutic demands more attentive listening than other interpretive methods, assumes biblical literacy, and succeeds as communication only if the congregation is predisposed to accept the specific analogy being made. Asking the political question here is more likely to motivate the already-convinced to action than to persuade the skeptical, because the analogy is not explicated or defended adequately.

For Elisabeth Schüssler Fiorenza, "getting down to cases" is described in terms of "a feminist hermeneutics of creative actualization." The Carlson sermon engages in creative actualization as it reformulates biblical vision and injunctions.[12] The biblical injunction in the Old Testament lesson was, "Choose this day whom you will serve;" in the Gospel lesson, *how* one serves is envisioned. What is not explicit in Carlson's sermon is how the actualization amplifies "feminist remnants that survive in patriarchal texts." The preacher names many current political issues, but does not identify feminist overtones in the text itself.

When Justo and Catherine Gonzalez write about the political concreteness of liberation interpretation, they place greater emphasis than Carlson and Schüssler Fiorenza on examining the way in which God intervenes or responds to the powerlessness of various individuals or groups of people.[13] Identifying oppression is a necessary first step; claiming God's advocacy normally comes next, followed by the announcement of divine liberation and invitation to participate in it. Were the Carlson sermon to address divine-human interaction as part of its political concreteness, it might have spoken more to what God does than what God wants. An invitation to the Eucharist shared by Christ is found in the conclusion, but Carlson focused most of her concrete analogy on the divine imperative from Deuteronomy: "keep the commandments and statutes of the Lord, which I command you this day for your good."

A second example of "getting down to cases" that conforms to the Gonzalez model (and some of Schüssler Fiorenza's concerns) more closely is Constance George's "A Resurrection Experience" in *Those Preaching Women*. Basing her sermon on John 20:11-18, George lifts up the experience of Mary Magdalene as paradigmatic for black women of the church:

> Mary went forth to prepare others for the assurance of a resurrection experience. Do you think she wanted to leave the presence of the risen Christ? Do you think she wanted to approach those frightened, beaten disciples? She was a woman. They would not believe her, was probably her first thought. But Mary had to go. Jesus had called her by name and sent her to tell them. . . . The women of our church have had a difficult journey in the last one hundred years—slavery, oppressive systems, cultural corruption, traditional rejections. Going into the next century we will need "a faith that will not shrink though pressed by many a foe." We need a faith like the mothers of the church exhibited.[14]

George's "creative actualization," like that of Sehested in the sermon on Shiphrah and Puah, brings to the forefront a powerless person of the time. Though Mary Magdalene is hardly unfamiliar, her role is re-envisioned in the sermon as equal to the apostles. The concrete analogy in the contemporary context loses none of the momentum of divine activity recorded in the text. The liberating word addresses a specific group of people in the present.

3. "Investigating a Story"

Perhaps the strongest affinity between feminist/liberation hermeneutics and preaching by women in general is the way both favor narrative/historical texts. By narrative/historical, I mean those pericopes that document actual events or present parable or story as events. Jesus healing ten lepers would be dealt with as history, but a small portion of Job's lament, unaccompanied by textual material putting in its historical context, would be treated as poetry. Justo and Catherine Gonzalez explain that liberation theology works with the category of history, and views the Bible primarily as the record of God's action in history rather than immutable essences or eternal laws.[15]

Narrative, prophetic, and parabolic texts lend themselves to this interpretive tool more readily than didactic or poetic material from the Bible. These latter categories are not beyond the reach of discerning divine action, however, if the preacher gives equal or greater attention to what may be known about the context of their composition. If one accepts the idea of biblical texts being self-consciously subject to feminist experience there is the possibility that texts which cannot be interpreted from a feminist/liberation perspective will be excised as patriarchal, mythical archetypes. The issue is then enlarged beyond liberation from patriarchy to the nature of canon in the Christian faith: a very controversial topic among feminists and nonfeminists.

Women preachers whose works have been published provide ample evidence of the predilection for historical or narrative pericopes.[16] They also show a tendency to give considerable information about the context in which a narrative text was written and how it might have been heard. By contrast, less than half the didactic, prophetic, and poetic texts demonstrate such insights. A strong example of "investigating a story" is found in "And Sarah Laughed: The Humor of God," by Yolande Herron-Palmore. The preacher uses a sermon structure that is familiar to the black church: exploring the text in some detail before exhorting the congregation in its particular needs. Sarah's predicament is presented not merely as a complication in a patriarchal story, but as worthy of consideration in its own right, and illustrative of God's challenge to have "the faith that makes things possible." During the first half of the message, the promise of God's liberating action in our own time is hinted at only in brief asides that appear on the surface as a device to maintain congregational interest:

> Many of us can identify with Sarah's action. We ask God to help us with our problems; then, when things don't happen as soon as seems to us urgently necessary, we take them back into our own little hands. . . . Sarah gradually became very jealous of Hagar and Ishmael, later forcing them to leave the household. We can identify with such complications, too . . . [Abraham] was limited by what he could see *now*. Many of us here have "seeing faith." We wouldn't dare ask God for anything we consider big. . . . We Christians of today also have many false understandings about faith. . . .[17]

In this sermon, the listener is encouraged to remember God's action as recorded in a narrative text, and rejoice that God continues to act in the listener's own context. Herron-Palmore does not challenge one obvious patriarchal bias in the text: God does not address Sarah directly, but tells her husband that Sarah will bear a son. The preacher does show feminist affinity in pointing out that the maleness of the promised child was crucial in a culture where only males could inherit property and be established as the ancestor of a great nation.

An even more explicit confluence of biblical narrative and feminist hermeneutics is found in "Woman as Oppressed; Woman as Liberated in the Scriptures," by Rosemary Radford Ruether. In this sermon, Hannah's hymn of praise, I Samuel 2:1-10 is compared with a New Testament canticle, Luke 1:47-55, but both are explicated as testimonies to God's liberating acts in human history. They are understood in their historical context.

> Mary's canticle thus clarifies the message of Hannah's canticle and carries us to a new level of understanding of God's messianic work in history. Salvation is not just reversal of fortunes, but is the ending of all unjust fortunes. This happens only when we seek out and identify with those who have been oppressed and despised in this present world.[18]

The texts for both of these sermons portray divinely-wrought change in the lives of women. It should be noted that (1) some feminist theologies have moved toward a theology of mutuality and solidarity, decrying the idea of an omnipotent and transcendent God as reinforcing patriarchal and ultimately oppressive stereotypes; (2) it is not necessary for a text to be about certain women in order to employ a feminist/liberation hermeneutic in interpretation.

4. "Reassigning the Cast of Characters"

Feminist interpreters maintain that the perspective of the powerless, particularly women, has been overlooked in the composition of Scripture and in the interpretation that takes place in proclamation. In western Christianity, preachers have a tendency to deal with prophetic texts by expounding from the (powerful) role of the prophet.[19] In making analogies to the present, the congregation then becomes whatever groups the prophet is addressing, directly or indirectly. Protected by the veil of "but this is what's happening in the text," the method allows the preacher to abuse power and vent anger in ways that may have little to do with the sermon text. Justo and Catherine Gonzalez suggest that a responsible preacher will "reassign the cast of characters" to allow the text to speak in a fresh way and give a voice to the powerless. Schüssler Fiorenza and Phyllis Trible demonstrate that women are routinely presented as powerless and voiceless in the Bible; therefore, reassigning the parts may facilitate an end to oppression.

The reassigning of parts normally consists of the preacher aligning herself with the congregation to be addressed by a prophetic voice. A sermon by Karolyn Edwards, based on Judges 19, surprised her congregation because the role that she assigned everyone present at worship, that of the people who received pieces of the dismembered concubine, was a vehicle of unexpected judgment. She wrote:

> "Consider, take counsel and speak," the Scripture says. To keep quiet is to sin. . . . To consider it is to reckon with the text, just as we have been doing. What we come up with is a text speaking loudly about mutilation of a woman, the blatant discounting of this misogyny only to further mutilate her body, to get revenge for damaged property. And considering her is to examine its implications for today—to look at the present reality of this text of terror. . . . The latest statistics report that one in every four females and one in every seven males will be sexually assaulted by the age of 18. . . . To take counsel on it is to say something about these realities. Try saying never again will I let that man beat me, abuse my child, hurt my family. Never again will I keep silent, pretending the violence just isn't there.[20]

Edwards forced the congregation to identify not with the nationalistic interests manifested in a patriarchal text, but with

99

those who were not shocked by violence against the powerless. The word spoke to and judged all in the congregation, but did not claim divine power or advocacy for the powerless.

In a sermon I preached on John 2:13-22, I attempted to reassign the cast of characters by resisting the temptation to identify with the disciples or crowd who saw Jesus drive the money changers from the temple. The worshipers were identified with the money changers in the story, and I aligned myself with them in being confronted by the text.

> It's not surprising we normally place ourselves with the Gospel writer as witnesses to rather than participants in the event. The world of first-century Judaism is still sufficiently remote and exotic that we have trouble standing in the sandals of those selling sheep and oxen. But in taking the perspective of observers rather than participants in the unfolding interaction between God and humanity, we endanger ourselves and our listeners by selling analogies that don't hold up under scrutiny. We stand under judgment when our sermons suggest that the only way people may receive God's truth is through what we demand they buy on Sunday morning. We become marketers of prejudice: anti-Semitism, spiritual elitism. . . .[21]

My experience of reading and listening to women's sermons suggests that women almost automatically adhere to the liberation theology tenet of "reassigning the cast of characters," perhaps due to the difference in perspective wrought by gender. Changing the congregation's point of identification with the text does not necessarily result in a liberating or "empowering" message, as I will demonstrate later in the chapter.

5. *"Preparing the Way"*

The fifth characteristic of liberation theology that is commonly found in women's preaching is the implicit assumption that the worshiping community's task is to move toward God's new social order, to work for it, to announce it, and to train for it.[22] Because God is the champion of the oppressed, and because of her predilection for historical/narrative texts, the preacher calls her congregation to cooperate with divine will and/or action as presently discerned, rather than conforming to ancient precept.

A woman taking a course in Wesleyan theology and preaching was assigned to write a sermon with Christian perfection as its emphasis. She chose Mark 12:28-34 as her text. She described sanctification not as a second work of grace accomplished by the Holy Spirit, but as a decision or commitment to be honored at any cost:

> Living a life in which we follow in the footsteps of Christ is to turn our whole person to God, once and for all, in a total obedience that renounces any competing loyalty. . . . When I live a life which has been transformed by God, I may be called to see the idolatry in the United States government and to call government policy to task when it is not following either the precepts of the country or the precepts of God, and I must obey God's law, for God's law is over all. It may mean as Christians and United Methodists we are called to work for socio-economic justice by trying to transform systems of oppression in which we participate.[23]

In a similar way, Barbara Brown Taylor, an Episcopal priest, used the story of Jesus and the Canaanite woman (Matthew 15:21-28) to point the way to God's new social order. Taylor's sermon differs from the one cited above in that the change called for within the listener is discussed as much as the change the listener works around him or her:

> The obvious interpretation [is] that we are surrounded by similar outcasts, equally lost causes, and that God calls us to expand our boundaries to include them, and to include the possibility that they may reach God's holy mountain ahead of us. . . . For us, it may be that part of ourselves that says we cannot really get close to anyone, that the old scars are too painful; or the part of us that says we can never measure up to what people expect of us . . . that kind of self-limitation is what today's gospel challenges, and challenges fiercely.[24]

In both sermons, the listeners are to be subjects and not merely objects of action. The sermon on Christian perfection focuses on human agency more than Taylor's message; this is not surprising, given that it is based on a pronouncement passage rather than a miracle story. Both women diagnose a problem and suggest its solution. Their sermons are forward-looking yet anchored in present concerns. In these ways, they are faithful to agendas common to liberation/feminist theologies.

Although the previous sermon excerpts demonstrate common ground between women's expositions of the Bible and liberation/feminist hermeneutics, they do not prove that the woman preacher is working from a deliberate feminist perspective. First, a woman does not have to regard the Bible and tradition as patriarchal articulation in order to bring a new perspective to the task of exegesis. The predilection toward preaching from historical/narrative texts is shared by women *and* men. It may be a by-product of using the suggested *Common Lectionary* texts or the considerable recent impact of Frederick Buechner and Garrison Keillor on the teaching of homiletics. The use of concrete analogy between the biblical context and the contemporary one did not begin with the emergence of liberation and feminist theologies, as a quick perusal of *Twenty Centuries of Great Preaching* will demonstrate. And the belief that the worship community's task is to move toward God's new social order is, among other things, a characteristic of liberalism in the United States earlier in this century. Finally, feminist assumptions about the nature of the canon are not representative of all women who preach. The use of one of these methodological tools, then, may or may not indicate the preacher's affinity with liberation/feminist interpretation.

OTHER CHARACTERISTICS OF WOMEN'S INTERPRETATION

Other characteristics of women's interpretive method in preaching do not necessarily reflect a particular theological or political position. The four that are identified in the following paragraphs may say more about women's psychological development and/or the way women are socialized in a western industrial culture than about deliberate hermeneutical method.

Immediate Amplification of Text

The first characteristic, which I have encountered more in preaching by younger women than in "second career" preachers, is immediate amplification of the text.[25] Sometimes the amplification deliberately heightens one aspect of the text, which the preacher will address later in the message. For example, a woman preaching on Jesus healing the lepers (Luke 17:11-19) used retelling of the text as a stepping-stone to confront certain problems in the pericope:

> There's something in this text that just doesn't seem to hold together. Maybe because I was an English major in college and trained to see things as a critic I'm being a bit harsh on Luke's parable. . . . So let's picture what's going on. Jesus is walking along the road, as he usually does, and a group of lepers call out to him from a distance—now this makes sense, because lepers had to maintain a certain distance from the rest of society—the law stated that a leper was unclean and could not come into the community. So they call out to him from a distance, "Lord, Master, have mercy on us." And he responds by saying, "Go show yourselves to the priests." But that doesn't make sense. The story starts falling apart for me. You see, in first century Palestine. . . .[26]

In a service of worship, the minister or liturgist had just finished reading the lesson, but the preacher chose to retell it in her own words. In the sermon on healing the ten lepers, introductory remarks prepared the congregation for amplification from a certain perspective, and for reasons they could understand. In other cases, however, the woman trying simultaneously to remain faithful to the text yet rephrasing it in her own words loses some listeners and alienates others. This is more likely to happen if her style of amplification is informal and/or her purpose is not clear. For example, a woman preaching on Ezekiel 37 said the following:

> While I was still speaking to the bones, I heard a noise coming from behind me. It started as a rustle, it grew into a rattle and a clanking! And so I looked over my shoulder to see what it might be. But dust

103

had so filled the air that I couldn't see, and as I stood there squinting, I heard the noise again, only this time in front of me. . . .[27]

In the second example amplification was followed by analogy to the present context. This can be very helpful to the congregation if the scripture reading itself is difficult or obscure. The preacher is giving them a second chance to understand it, using more familiar language and "standing with them" in their uncertainty in a collegial way.

The preacher must exercise a balance of imagination and self-discipline, so that the metaphors she uses engage her congregation rather than distracting or merely entertaining them. Unfortunately, the texts that seem to get amplified are not unfamiliar, puzzling ones, but stories the listeners could retell themselves. In addition, amplification sometimes does not display the fruits of the preacher's exegetical work in her study, and its absence may be another point of resistance among listeners. Their discomfort has several bases; if the same text was presented during the "children's time," for example, the sermon may be the third recitation of the text from the preacher's lips. Some in the congregation will be simultaneously attentive and resistant, suspecting the preacher of modifying the story to serve whatever analogies she wants to make. During the sermon on Ezekiel, the congregation was not given a framework for understanding what happened to the prophet or how the story was heard in its original context; the listeners only learned how the preacher felt about the text.

Another type of interpretation by amplification used by women is line-by-line exposition of the text. It is a method that enjoyed greater popularity in other periods of church history. Today it tends to be used most in the independent (nondenominational) evangelical tradition, among males who have great charismatic leadership skills, and whose authority in the congregation rests on their role as Bible teacher during Sunday worship and midweek services. The method is less common among male clergy in contemporary mainline denominations. Staying close to the words and apparent intent of the text and including substantial exegetical insights may be one way for the woman preacher to establish credibility where it might otherwise be challenged. A woman writing her first sermon provides an example of this method:

> "When it grew late he was there by Himself, while the boat was by now a long way from the shore at the mercy of the waves, for the wind was dead against them." While Jesus was in prayer, the disciples found themselves struggling with the wind and the waves. They had obeyed Christ, but even so they were in trouble, as sudden storms on the sea of Galilee were common. . . .[28]

The development of such a sermon follows the direction of the text and tends to be linear, rather than building up to a climax or strong sense of conclusion. As in the other type of interpretation by amplification, line-by-line exposition is a useful method if the biblical text is an unfamiliar and puzzling one. Congregations can become accustomed to listening to this method of interpretation, though it means sermon (and worship service) length is at the mercy of the length of the text being explicated.

Identifying with the Least Powerful

A second characteristic of women's interpretation, alluded to earlier in "reassigning the cast of characters," are the tendencies to identify with the least powerful person in a narrative text, invite congregational identification, and interpret the story from that perspective. Virtually every time I have heard a woman preach on Luke 10:38-42, the preacher has invited identification with Mary and/or Martha, whether placing the characters in the pericope in the contemporary context or encouraging the congregation to enter the original context of the story. It is not uncommon for the woman preacher to "take on" Martha's name to interpret the text from her perspective:

> We don't know what Martha did then. We don't know if she walked out of the kitchen and sat down in her rocking chair and never lifted a finger again. . . . We have no idea if this

conversation changed Martha or what impact it had on her life. But I can tell you about what happened to MarthaShelley.[29]

By contrast, the male preacher interpreting the same text is likely to go straight to the pronouncement by Jesus and explicate it for the congregation, that is, assume the voice of the "powerful" in the text, and speak from that perspective. The male preacher is more apt to tell the congregation what they should do rather than who they are.

It is not surprising that a woman preacher would identify with a positive feminine example in the Bible. However, the point of identification seems to be not related to gender, but to powerlessness. A second example, from a sermon on Mark 10:46-52 by Margaret W. Crockett-Cannon, had an introduction that could have led to identification with Jesus the healer, but moved instead to interpretation from the perspective of Bartimaeus:

> Recently I was talking with a friend whose body is marked with the losses and scars of many radical operations. When she learned I was serving as a chaplain in a hospital, she told me of a time when she was very ill and thought she was going to die. . . . Jesus does with us as he did with Bartimaeus. Jesus asks us to look at our true hopes and express them, to profess our faith so that he can act on that faith. . . .[30]

If the preacher uses identification with the less powerful in the text as an interpretive method, she may effectively grant permission for listeners to be similarly vulnerable. A congregation that understands itself as powerless in some way will find this method of interpretation both liberating and comforting. If the preacher consistently uses this method of exposition, however, the congregation may perceive it as begging for affirmation or lacking conviction. It can foster passivity if the preacher portrays herself and the congregation solely as objects of action rather than initiators of it or participants in God's gracious initiative. It should also be noted that this "reassigning the cast of characters" functions in a way contrary to liberation hermeneutics. The underdogs in the text assume a degree of blame for their predicament. No villains are responsible for their suffering, and the appropriate responses to divine intervention in the story are: (1) to give thanks; and (2) to re-examine what changes the "oppressed" need to make in their lives.

Focusing on Relationship

A third characteristic of women's interpretive method is choosing to focus on the dynamics of relationship evidenced in the text, and preach a sermon that works for reconciliation in divine-human and interpersonal relationships. At times, this exegetical method raises questions about possible avoidance of more difficult issues in the text. A sermon on Matthew 14:22-33 demonstrates equilibrium in relationships as interpretive bias:

> It probably hurt Peter quite a bit when he was accused of having little faith by Jesus as he attempted to walk on the water. . . . Can you picture Jesus as he looked into Peter's eyes as he spoke to him? How would *you* feel having Jesus look into your eyes, saying, "I have prayed for you. . . ." Peter must have felt his heart being warmed. . . .[31]

For this preacher, who identified strongly with Peter, being able to hold Jesus' hand was everything. The illustrations in the sermon all pertained to the themes of fear, alienation, and assurance of reconciliation. The avoidance previously mentioned was manifested in sermon structure as well as content; though the preacher did a verse-by-verse exposition of the text, she skipped verse 25: "And in the fourth watch of the night he came to them, walking on the sea"—suggesting she didn't want to affirm or deny the existence of miracles; relationship was the key issue for her.

The importance of relationship was also mentioned by E. Claiborne Jones, when discussing a sermon preached at Holy Innocents' Episcopal Church in Atlanta. She described preaching from the top of the sanctuary steps in a fan-shaped, large, yet intimate eucharistic room, where preaching seemed like an "oddly personal conversation with four hundred folks." Her sermon, based on Matthew 18:21-35, began with an autobiographical anecdote about returning to this church, and then proceeded to tell them her mother had just undergone cancer surgery. The relationships between the preacher and her mother, the preacher and former schoolmates, and a backslider and the congregation are explored in the light of the relationship in the text between the king and the debtors.[32]

My conviction is that the predilection to interpret texts in terms of achieving equilibrium in relationships is not a conscious decision made by women preachers, but reflects Gilligan's and Eriksson's assertion that feminine identity is awakened or established in a relationship of intimacy with another person.[33] In the same vein, Nancy Chodorow wrote that in a culture where the mother is primary caregiver, the development of a boy child's masculinity is dependent on separation, where a girl child's femininity depends on attachment to her mother: "Because of their mothering by women, girls come to experience themselves as less separate than boys, as having more permeable ego boundaries. Girls seem to define themselves more in relation to others."[34]

In *Women's Ways of Knowing,* the tendency of women to identify themselves in terms of relationships to others (or by severing those relationships) is seen as a stage in women's development. In a discussion with other women who teach homiletics about the prevalence of "relational" interpretive method among women, there was no argument that this is a recurring characteristic, but disagreement as to its cause. Some attribute the popularity of this method to the way women are enculturated in a patriarchal society; therefore, while the method itself is neither bad nor good, a woman preacher must be made aware of the misogynic social structure that positively reinforces women who use this "feminine" method. Others thought the orientation toward relationship-oriented cognitive processes (including biblical interpretation) is something with which females are born—regardless of the culture. My own view is somewhere between these two points, and that the legitimacy of this interpretive tool is determined by asking: (1) whether it reflects the apparent intentionality of the text, and (2) whether it is likely to be an effective communication method in the context in which the woman will preach.

The Preacher's Internal Authority

The final method of interpretation that is common among women preachers is to address and evaluate the text from the perspective of the preacher's internal authority, based on her own experiences. This is not quite the same phenomenon as using autobiographical illustrations—something both men and women do in various ways. Nor is it identical to the method of feminist exegesis proposed by Christine Smith: taking women's experience as the starting point for a hermeneutic of suspicion; the "internal authority" ends as well as starts with the dictates of the inner voice. At its best, it reflects honest struggle between the preacher's reality and the challenge of the text, and legitimates the working of the Holy Spirit in individuals and community as well as in the Word. At its worst, this method suggests exegetical narcissism, disallows semantic autonomy of the passage under consideration, and communicates itself as "how I felt about this text." Mary Field Belenky discusses this kind of internal authority in this way:

> When women are just beginning to make the transition into subjectivism, they are no longer willing to rely on higher status, powerful authorities in the public domain for knowledge and truth. Instead they consider turning for answers to people closer to their own experiences—female peers, mothers, sisters, grandmothers. . . . Truth for these transitional women is particular and grounded in the firsthand experience of others most like themselves. . . . Truth resides within the person and can negate answers that the outside world supplies.[35]

An example of the preacher's internal authority used as interpretive tool is in this excerpt of a sermon based on Exodus 20:8-11:

> For many of us "remembering the sabbath day" carries with it a connotation of legalism; it is one of those "laws" that has become obsolete for our day. . . . Why is it too hard for us to observe a sabbath day? My guess is that it has to do with fear. Fear of silence,

fear of stillness, fear of God's revelation. . . . It is necessary to take a sabbath because without it, our wellspring of the Spirit runs dry.[36]

There is nothing startling in what the preacher says about the Sabbath; it is what is unsaid that suggests a self-ratified hermeneutic. The pericope used for the sermon is part of the Ten Commandments, which Judaism and Christianity understand as divine imperatives given to God's covenant people. But apart from an aside in the second paragraph, nothing is said about these words as God's command. The authority of the text communicated to the congregation resides in the judgment of the preacher. The message appeals to the community's concurrence with her experience.

This interpretive standpoint is also suggested in Peggy Way's sermon, "You Are Not My God, Jehovah." Making explicit reference to her text, Romans 8:28-39 in the last third of the sermon, her message begins with an affirmation clearly rooted in her own experience:

You are not my God, Jehovah!!!
I will speak with my brother.
I will affirm my sisters.
I will cry unto my God: let us free one another. . . .
I will not serve a god for whom woman was unclean for twice as long when she bore a girl child. . . . or a god for whom a woman's mission is to listen and a man's mission to speak.[37]

The preacher's feminist identity is indicated in the declarations concerning specifically misogynist passages in the Bible. "Internal authority," however, is suggested by the unexplicated, emphatic statement with which the sermon begins, and by the sentiment that people will free one another and, quite possibly, the preacher and God will free one another. Truth, in this sermon, resides most clearly in the preacher's own person.

HERMENEUTICAL STRATEGIES THAT WORK

Most congregations are better able to describe recurrent themes or perhaps usual structure in their pastor's preaching than the finer

110

points of hermeneutics. Their evaluative comments on the relationship of text to sermon can be summed up by one of the following: (1) the sermon was faithful to the text; (2) the preacher manipulated the text for his/her own purposes; (3) the sermon didn't seem to have much to do with the text. Given the abundance of hermeneutical methods available and the fairly basic criteria by which the congregation judges fidelity to the text, what strategies best serve the woman preacher in interpretation?

First, the preacher will do well to remember that whatever her theological orientation, her sermon involves interpretation not only of a text but also of a congregation and its perception of itself and of her. Furthermore, most worshipers listen and participate better on Sunday morning if there is a degree of familiarity and continuity with what they have experienced there before. Any radically new and different method of proclaiming a text—feminist or otherwise—is likely to put them on guard. For this reason, a woman is wise not to employ an explicit feminist hermeneutic for shock value while preaching to people for whom this method is unfamiliar. It will arouse premature resistance and sabotage successful communication of the point of her sermon. A stronger strategy is to interpret the congregation in advance, consider their self-understanding and needs, and work with these in a subtle way.

Rosemary Radford Ruether employed this strategy when preaching one Ascension Sunday at Duke University Chapel. It was reasonable to assume that one of the country's best-known feminist theologians and a congregation in conservative North Carolina had preconceived notions about each other. Ruether began her message in an engaging, nonconfrontational way by acknowledging the liturgical season. She then moved directly to the text, reminding the congregation of events that occurred just before and after those described in the reading for that morning. Her thesis was the question of where the church finds the locus of Christ's presence, now that the risen Savior is not among us in the flesh.[38] Only at that point did she introduce political and theological questions of how the institutional church gradually placed artificial limitations on Christ's presence, for example, prohibiting the leadership of women. Her feminist hermeneutic became evident only later in the sermon, after the congregation had given assent to ideas already presented.

Second, the preacher should keep in mind that liberation hermeneutics (with or without a feminist slant) are a "better fit" with some texts than with others. Liberation theology focuses on the Bible as history, and tends to view this history in terms of tension between oppressors and oppressed. Although liberation theologians assert that this hermeneutic is not something the preacher "tries on" occasionally, that it must be an unwavering commitment expressed in every sermon, I believe not all of Scripture lends itself to these interpretive tools.

What about a woman preacher's tendency to identify with the least powerful person in a narrative text? As noted earlier, this can be used to enable the congregation to be addressed by the text in new and often exciting ways. The preacher will do well to contemplate the affinity or discrepancy between her own "way of knowing" the text and her congregation's experience of it, and going one step further, the possibilities and limitations of shifting perspectives. A black congregation listening to a Good Friday sermon, for example, may wonder what is amiss if the preacher speaks from the perspective of "Veronica," a name some traditions give to one of the women who watched Jesus on his way to Calvary. Their point of identification with the text is likely to be with the One who suffered on the cross for others, and if the cast of characters is being reassigned, they will expect interpretation to occur from that perspective.

Finally, the advisability of using "relationship" as an interpretive starting point depends not only on the text, but also on the size of the congregation and the way the woman interacts with worshipers during the rest of the service. Relational interpretation may be therapeutic as well as shedding new light on a text in large congregations, where there isn't much else going for intimacy or a sense of community. It invites listeners to draw their own analogies between the world of the text and their own. A preacher should not substitute this homiletical method for creation and nurturing of community in the rest of the life of the church. In employing this method of approaching a text and suggesting its application to listeners, the preacher should also beware of "squishiness," pretending a kind of intimacy that does not exist and/or frustrating those for whom equilibrium in relationship is not the most pressing issue presented in the text.

*I*t is virtually impossible for a woman in our culture to preach without making a decision for or against inclusive language, because no woman becomes a preacher without encountering resistance, real and/or projected, on the basis of gender.

*F*or these feminists, it is not just a matter of saying, "God the Father *and* Mother," but asking whether the imbalance of power reflected in a parent-child relationship is the best metaphor for describing the divine-human relationship.

*I*n order for new imagery (or usage) to take hold with integrity and staying power, it must be intelligible to the community in which it is spoken, and it also must read correctly the metaphor it seeks to replace. Women preachers should beware of universalizing women's experience just as men in the pulpit ought to reexamine the male-oriented, hierarchical language they may be using.

*W*omen's evocative language, rich with adjectives and adverbs, is opaque or turgid if it is missing the directive element that worshipers expect from a leader of worship. . . . The community's solidarity will be built on shared frustration or boredom if, lacking a common frame of reference, the preacher denies them the means to organize the impressionistic images offered during the sermon.

S I X

THEOLOGY IN METAPHOR AND GRAMMAR

Students in my introductory preaching course often assume that the class session on "language" will be solely an attempt to "sell" them on the merits of inclusive language about God and humanity. Though inclusiveness is an important issue for women preachers, women are not the only ones interested in it. In addition, it is only one of several issues worthy of attention when considering women's vocabulary and syntax in the pulpit.

Three aspects of language will be considered in the following pages. The first is theological language, which takes in the question of inclusiveness. The second question concerns the use of "intuitive" or "expressive" language verses "directive" language in communication. The third issue is the way a woman preacher's syntax reinforces or undermines authority and credibility in the pulpit.

It is necessary to use different media in examining these issues. Published sermons, which have been edited and refined by the author, disclose a woman preacher's intent in employing some theological metaphors and not using others. The self-conscious decision for or against inclusive language is also evident, disclosing her hope of reshaping the faith and understanding of the reader. But printed sermons are usually not a good medium for revealing a woman preacher's predilection toward expressive or instrumental language, or her syntax in verbal communication. They are expressed with less self-consciousness and intentionality, and are manifested more frequently in oral communication from sermon notes. Though they play a significant role in shaping the way the sermon is heard, these nuances tend to be edited out of sermon manuscripts before they are circulated.

Why focus on these particular issues? It would certainly be possible to write an entire book on metaphors for God used in contemporary women's sermons. Sermon structure might be another avenue worth exploring under the heading of theology in metaphor and grammar. However, I chose three issues that recurred in my preaching courses. They are worth pursuing because they deal not only with gender per se, but also with power and autonomy. They have ramifications for women's interaction with church members outside the context of worship as well as women's communication from the pulpit.

THEOLOGICAL LANGUAGE IN PREACHING AND LITURGY

Inclusiveness

In the first part of this section, dealing with inclusiveness in theological language, it is not my purpose to recapitulate all that has been written by contemporary feminists (and nonfeminists) on the subject. The focus is rather on examination of the predominant ways in which concern for inclusive language manifests itself in preaching by women. This is accompanied by an explication of the theological assumptions supporting each pattern of usage.

It is virtually impossible for a woman in our culture to preach without making a decision for or against inclusive language, because no woman becomes a preacher without encountering resistance, real and/or projected, on the basis of gender. One common way of dealing with the issue is to employ inclusive language about humanity while maintaining traditional and familiar language about divinity. This has been the route taken by numerous hymnal revision committees as well as women preachers in traditions with a strong view of the authority of the Bible. For example, in a sermon on Luke 24:44-53 and Acts 1:1-11, a woman who teaches homiletics wrote:

And now, here we are at the end of the trail; our Lord has taken
leave of us. He came into our lives as the infinite love of God, bent
down to find all us lost children. But now he returns to the Father
whence he came, and we have reached the end of his earthly story.[1]

In a similar way, contemporary preaching by black women
frequently uses traditional masculine language about God, but
inclusive language about humanity:

Calling on the name of Jesus isn't like calling on any other name.
You may exercise a little power over another human when you call
out their name . . . [Jesus is] demonstrating his claim to be *the* Son
of God . . . I know a man, sent from God, who's told me all about
myself. I know a man who set me free from the darkened dungeon
of despair.[2]

What theological assumptions inform a decision to use language
this way? It is reasonable to conclude that these preachers are
comfortable with traditional masculine language about God, since
they not only use metaphors and epithets found in Scripture, but
also use masculine pronouns. The absence of new metaphors and
images suggests, but does not prove, a fairly conservative
understanding of biblical authority. Language about humanity that
is not gender-specific leads one to believe the preachers are aware
of the issue of inclusiveness. The lack of evidence for a feminist
"hermeneutic of suspicion" allows speculation that the preachers
do not sympathize with that hermeneutic or that they regard it as of
secondary importance to other, more pressing theological issues.
These two samples do not address the frequent tension between
inclusiveness and authority issues pertaining to Scripture and
tradition. This question is addressed in the chapter on women's
interpretation of Scripture as well as further on in this section.

What is likely to be the congregational response to this use of
language? My own experience suggests the following:

1. Unless they know something about these two preachers
beforehand (and have preconceived expectations), listeners are not

likely to notice their inclusive language about humans in the sermon itself. Some would be more likely to notice exclusive language.

2. If the woman in the pulpit changes the language about humans in familiar texts to make it more inclusive, some in the average congregation will notice, and some will not.

3. The masculine language about divinity will be noticed by some, but not all in the congregation. Even those who favor inclusive language about God are less put off by masculine language about the second person of the Trinity than the first person. This is because the Jesus of history did take on the form of a human male, whereas the "Father" did not.

A second group of women preachers and theologians believe the prevalence of masculine images in religious language is the result of the ungodly patriarchy that has plagued the church for centuries. Faithful preaching, for them, means refraining from using any masculine names or metaphors for divinity. Ian Ramsey's *Religious Language,* first published in 1963, is sometimes cited as contributing to feminist understanding of the nature of patriarchal language. Ramsey examined the peculiar categories of religious language: attempts to articulate or evoke that which is ultimately beyond language. In his section on "models and qualifiers," he suggested that ordinary words without necessarily religious connotations function as "models" that transform the subject into the divine when modified by a qualifier.[3] He gives the examples of "Father" and "Lord" as models that gain religious significance when qualified by "Eternal" and "of all life."

Feminist theologians who approach religious language with Ramsey's frame of reference find the practice of calling God "heavenly Father" or "eternal Father" intolerable, for it suggests that maleness is central to God's identity. According to feminist Virginia Mollenkott, the unconscious mind is exceedingly literal, and the messages we send to it by the imagery we use concerning God are taken very literally. Furthermore, she calls the resulting assumption that God is actually Father an unconscious idolatry.[4] The masculine religious language represented by models and

118

qualifiers has also been blamed for the mistreatment of women in the church by regarding them as invisible or by overt oppression.[5]

Many sermons preached from this understanding of language manifest a dearth of terms of divinity. The names and metaphors for God are few, unevocative, and one-dimensional. For example, in a sermon by Professor Letty Russell, published in 1974, "God" is the only designation for the first person of the Trinity, though richer language about the second person of the Trinity is given in biblical citations:

> Service is God's gift because it is God who serves us. Think of it. This God of the Hebrew-Christian tradition is like no other gods! . . . In God's service, we see what Karl Barth calls the humanity of God . . . the humanity of God is seen in that God chooses to be related to human beings through service.[6]

In the same way, in a sermon by a black Baptist woman, the abandonment of models and qualifiers resulted in self-conscious, unevocative prose:

> But God works in a mysterious way. God is good, but God will permit things to happen to us in order to bring to our awareness the source of our blessings. . . . Eventually, however, God will remind us that God is the benefactor we've been taking for granted. So in this text, God told Elijah to tell Ahab that God was sending a famine.[7]

What theological assumptions do these preachers communicate here? Their word choice suggests that language is a tool too quickly turned into a weapon against women and against the feminine aspects of the divine nature. The integrity of the proclaimed Word is protected by vigilance against patriarchy. Faithfulness requires the woman preacher to "play it safe" by choosing language that is uncontroversial and bland. The average congregation might "hear" the following in these language patterns:

1. They are more likely to hear the woman preacher's attempt to be inclusive, since the absence of personal and reflexive

119

pronouns is a variation from normal English speech patterns (ex.: God will remind us that God . . .).

2. If the variation from familiar speech patterns becomes too pronounced (ex.: God gave God's promise to God's people . . .), the congregation may believe that inclusive language is the sermon topic, regardless of the woman preacher's intention. The speech pattern may be subject to ridicule.

3. Feminists in the congregation will be encouraged by a preacher who takes their concerns seriously. They will listen appreciatively to whatever else the preacher says.

4. Given the absence of models and qualifiers or other evocative language about divinity, the congregation will have a more difficult time thinking or talking about divine nature and actions later on. This is because they have been given minimal linguistic tools for the task.

I believe that for some feminist women, the absence of models and qualifiers is a transitional stage in the reshaping of religious language. The examples drawn from Russell and Mollenkott are from older anthologies of women's sermons. With the passing of time and/or more experience in preaching, women who eschew "models and qualifiers" seem to develop in one of three directions. The first group of women preachers appears to move away from *all* religious language, so that interpersonal and intrapersonal concerns become the foci of their sermons. The second group of preaching women adopt or cultivate new model and qualifier forms for their proclamation. Feminists in the third group introduce feminine models to balance the prevalence of masculine religious language already in use, or suggest divine androgyny. Of course, the evolution of some women's language overlaps these boundaries.

Two examples from Rosemary Radford Ruether's work illustrate the first trajectory of change. In a 1974 sermon on Matthew 23:1-12, "You Shall Call No Man Father," Ruether focused on interpersonal relationships more than divine-human.[8] There were no "models and qualifiers" used in the sermon. When the historical Jesus was under discussion and a pronoun was unavoidable, Ruether used "he." When God was referred to as "he" in the scripture reading, she did not change it, and, surprisingly, the phrase "Kingdom of God" found its way into the concluding paragraphs. Ruether identified metaphors used in the New Testament that were misappropriated to support misogyny, but did not deal with the issue of God-language directly. Changes in Ruether's language are demonstrated in her 1985 book, *Women-Church*. Divinity is referred to as God/ess. The liturgies by Ruether and others manifest a decrease in specifically religious language, while not doing away with metaphorical theology. Part of the eucharistic liturgy is as follows:

> *Blessing of the Cup:* We are the new wine of life that flows in the branches of the vinetree. We remember our brother Jesus, who poured out his blood to water the roots of his vine. We also remember the many brothers and sisters who have died that a new world might be born: Oscar Arnulfo Romero, Martin Luther King, Ita Ford, Dorothy Kazal. . . .[9]

The search for language about divinity that is "faithful and fair" appears resolved for Ruether. The focus of discussion in this ritual and others is on the creation and maintenance of human communities working for justice and liberation.

The second trajectory of change is from absence of models and qualifiers to cultivation of new ones. Many denominational agencies offer lists of names, titles, and phrases purported to be free of masculine bias. Some language is drawn from the Bible; other words are the product of contemporary imagination. Most of the following are drawn from a resource prepared for the Board of Discipleship of The United Methodist Church:

Awesome One	Lover of Peace
Binder of Wounds	Refuge and Strength
Ceaseless Working	Heart's Delight
Existence Itself	Overhanging Tree
Mind of the Universe	Total Mystery
Ultimate One	Upholder of the Falling
Comfort of Sufferers	Shelter from the Storm

121

Isabel Carter Heyward provides an example of how new models and qualifiers, both original and borrowed, may be incorporated into the sermon in an intelligible and colorful way:

> There, and there only perhaps, are we likely to be encountered by the Holy One of Israel, whom Jesus called abba (daddy) and who, in truth, is also the Mother of us all, the Source of our Birth, the Wellspring of Love in History, the Root of all Justice—and Compassion; always veiled, hid from full view, perceptible only to eyes of faith.[10]

Though the new metaphors are not explicated in the course of the sermon, their appearance in conjunction with more traditional language results in their fulfilling an evocative and doxological role.

In *Prayer on Wings,* other guidelines are offered for developing metaphors for worship. The process of discerning appropriate language is different from Ramsey's "model and qualifier" model:

> When we consider the effect that using various metaphors has upon our self-respect, we might tend to choose some metaphors which definitely produce a feeling of "likeness," identification. . . . While the Goddess metaphor affirms the female body in all of its stages, other feminine metaphors will evoke the affirmation of the body in particular stages. . . . Woman between puberty and menopause may find affinity and closeness with the Deity as Bleeding Goddess, one who can affirm the goodness of monthly bleeding, yet who can know the pain, worries, and ambiguities it evokes. . . . [others describe] the comfort they receive thinking of themselves or their loved ones rocked in the arms of a Grandmother God.[11]

This discussion of religious language both utilizes the model and qualifier combination and encourages development of feminine imagery to balance masculine metaphors used in corporate and individual prayer. In this regard *Prayer on Wings* shares common ground with the third strand coming from the initial awareness of overwhelmingly masculine names and epithets for God. However, there is an important difference between the author's understanding of authority and tradition in the cultivation of religious language and that of the group represented by the editors of *An Inclusive Language Lectionary*, Nancy Hardesty, Gail Ramshaw, and others. In *Prayer on Wings*, the church's tradition is consulted as one of *many* resources to be considered in searching for prayer language. Materials from *The Gnostic Gospels*, TM, New Age and Goddess theology are quoted alongside orthodox writings without evaluative comment. There is little sense of mutual accountability in the discernment process, except for the feelings of those present in worship when a particular metaphor is used.

What distinguishes the third trajectory of change in women preachers' movement toward more inclusive language about divinity? It is explicit and unapologetic in its rootedness in the historic community of faith. *An Inclusive Language Lectionary*, for example, does not do away with the term "Father" in reference to God, but where "God the Father" appears in a lectionary reading, the editors revise it to read "God the Father [and Mother]." Revisions in gender-specific language were made when this was supportable by original Greek and Hebrew texts.[12] In this lectionary, both Yahweh and Adonai are rendered God or Sovereign, and "Father," especially when it does not modify "God," is treated as a metaphor rather than a name for God. In a similar way, biblical feminist Nancy Hardesty does not call for the elimination of "certain traditional beloved forms of language," but suggests that preachers expand and enrich their vocabularies rather than further restricting them.[13] Her sermon, "Just as I Am," provides an example of using a greater variety of biblical images and metaphors for God:

> In [Isaiah] chapter 49, verse 15, God declares: "Can a woman forget her sucking child, that she should have no compassion on the [child] of her womb? Even these may forget, yet I will not forget you." . . . Isaiah speaks of a God who gathers sons and daughters from the ends of the earth; Jesus speaks of a God who sweeps the entire house looking for that one lost coin, that one lost soul. . . . We are made by God in God's image. We are icons of God, the only living representations of God.[14]

It should be noted that Hardesty uses only two names for divinity (Jesus and God) although a number of metaphors and images are used. The previously mentioned sermon by Isabel Carter Heyward, "Learning to See," offers another example of "expanded vocabulary," drawing upon the Bible and Christian tradition to balance masculine and feminine images for God.

Most women who conform to this pattern of usage regard inclusive language about humanity as a given. When the preacher speaks about God, however, inclusiveness is only one of a constellation of issues to be taken into account. For example, trinitarian dogma, christological centrality, and biblical warrant take precedence over gender issues.[15] Any choice of words that does not take these other criteria into account is found wanting. There is also the assumption that the woman in the pulpit can exercise her religious imagination more in the sermon than in liturgical prayer. The "expanded vocabulary" employed by women of this persuasion is used to assist in teaching and preaching, but not in speaking *to* God. For example, a woman preaching on the parable of the Prodigal Son may liken God both to a welcoming father and a nurturing mother, but is not likely to address God as Mother in corporate prayer. Liturgical scholar Gail Ramshaw explains the rationale for this:

> Some feel that Christianity can be both orthodox and feminist . . . [urging] the use of "In the name of God, the mother and father of all life. . . ." But the Christian God is related to the worshiper through adoption by faith, not through ownership by creation.[16]

In addition, addressing God as Father *and* Mother suggests that the deity is hermaphroditic, an idea contrary to catholic tradition. Further problems arise when trinitarian language is altered:

> The substitution of Parent for Father absolutely contradicts the shocking personal revelation of God by Jesus; and somehow the Spirit must remain the Spirit of the risen Christ. Creator, Redeemer, Sustainer is a contemporary reincarnation of modalism which naively equates one function each to one person each, an

idea wholly denied by classical theology . . . [and] it skirts the
central question in the naming of God: who is Jesus in relation to
God?[17]

To what extent will the average congregation notice and respond
to the woman preacher's language choice, if her own homiletical
development follows one of these three trajectories? This may
depend more on the liturgical orientation of the church than its
feminist sensitivities. However, the following general observations can be made:

1. Churches with a strong liturgical identity will be more
resistant to altered trinitarian formulas than congregations in the
free church tradition.

2. Listeners are more sensitive to the preacher changing
personal pronouns pertaining to God than to her avoidance of
pronouns.

3. Worshipers will be more amenable to an "expanded
vocabulary" used by the woman preacher than to changing the
words in familiar hymns and prayers.

4. A woman preacher whose concern for inclusiveness leads to
few names or metaphors for God, or diminished attention to the
divine-human relationship in her sermons, is likely to encounter
mixed reactions from the congregation. Some listeners will
appreciate her increased focus on interpersonal and intrapersonal
issues. Others will experience dissatisfaction that the sermons
"aren't religious enough."

5. Listeners with a strong feminist identity will resist the
woman preacher whose basis for language choice is trinitarian
dogma, liturgical tradition, or biblical warrant rather than
contemporary women's consciousness.

Selection and Creation of Metaphors

Some preachers have been asked to go over their sermon
manuscripts and list all the names, metaphors, and epithets for
God they have used. Then they are to identify the most important

words in the sermon's main idea, and list all the synonyms and paraphrases used for the key words. Most preachers are chagrined at how brief, dull, and unengaging their lists are, particularly when compared with the abundance of metaphorical language found in hymns and songs based on their sermon texts and in Scripture itself. There are, for instance, as many as ninety-six different images for the church found in the New Testament.[18]

The religious metaphors found in Scripture, hymnals, or other published works reflect a certain *range* of analogies and evocative words: a range that is usually limited by the world view, experiences, and concerns of those who authored them. For example, in the nineteenth century the advent of travel by locomotive—an amazing innovation at the time—stirred the religious imagination of lyricists who then wrote gospel songs such as "Life's Railway to Heaven," and "The Grand Excursion." The excitement, power, and apprehension associated with travel by rail were likened to the Christian's journey through life and death to the Kingdom of Heaven. God the Father became the Superintendent, Jesus the one who had purchased one-way tickets for all who believed, and travelers were advised to "keep your hand upon the throttle and your eye upon the rail." The evocative power of this constellation of metaphors diminished as trains became more commonplace (and were eclipsed by other forms of transportation) and the gospel songs based on these metaphors were no longer used.

Because language is a reflection of an individual's experience as well as one's tradition, and most preachers (until recently) were male, it was not surprising that congregations would encounter new metaphors and imagery when the individual whose experience it reflected was female. Women have raised questions about the range of enlivening and metaphorical language they have inherited from their church and culture. Their concern is related to the issue of inclusiveness but is not limited to gender-related imagery. Their presence invites the church as a whole to consider the methods used to decide what metaphors and imagery best convey the truth of the gospel.

Challenging existing metaphorical language and creating new

models is usually a self-conscious act. Many feminists believe that the traditional ways of naming God in concepts and abstract definitions are inadequate for women preachers. Because of their commitment to inclusiveness in every aspect of Christian faith, they call for new faith-language that values female experience and therefore transforms patriarchal, oppressive religious models.[19] For these feminists, it is not just a matter of saying, "God the Father *and* Mother," but asking whether the imbalance of power reflected in a parent-child relationship is the best metaphor for describing the divine-human relationship. In the same vein, language about divine sovereignty and creation might be reevaluated by the preacher who is concerned about the threat of nuclear annihilation. Instead of images of power evoked in Creator-creation terminology, she might identify the world as a sacramental sign of God's vulnerability and presence.[20]

In *Metaphorical Theology,* Sallie McFague writes that theological models tend to order rather than discover things. The models are related to one another hierarchically, and affect the feelings and actions of those who use them.[21] Responsible selection or creation of metaphors for the contemporary church, then, involves a critique of the way such language has functioned until now. It means not only heeding the voices that have been heard in the past, but also contextualizing theological discourse so that it reflects authentically the experience of those who use it in the present.[22]

How does this find expression when women preach? What I have discovered is that women select and develop metaphors more conservatively in their preaching than in the liturgies they create. "Grandmother Gods" and "Awesome Ones" are few and far between in homilies. The experience-based images that appear in women's sermons are likely to be familiar models serving a different purpose. For example, a woman preaching on Genesis 6:5-8; 7:10-12 transformed a metaphor for divine punishment into a vehicle of self-renewal:

> Now let's look at the symbolic meaning of the word *flood* and see how it applies to you and me. Many of us go through our daily

experience harboring in our minds any number of negative thoughts. . . . Now what am I saying? Simply that all these experiences I've just cited need to be flooded. . . . If you really want a flood in your life, then right now, right where you are, release the negativity and ask for the flood of the Spirit and of the living God to wash you and make you clean.[23]

In this case, the metaphor was created through allegorical interpretation of a particular biblical event. The dominant image in the sermon was drawn from the text. In other cases, women combine traditional theological concepts with images not having intrinsic theological meaning. A sermon on Mark 8:31-37 demonstrates this:

What dance is this? It is the dance of discipleship! And it is Christ who is our partner who draws us into the dance, Christ who urges us forward when we would step backward, Christ who by our side fears his cross as much as we fear ours, yet who moves forward into the dance with danger. It is our love for Christ our partner that keeps us going on.[24]

When the image of dance is found in the Bible, it is a metaphor for rejoicing and praise. Unlike "the Flood," dance is not associated with a particular time or place in Scripture. The woman who wrote this sermon borrowed dance as a metaphor for discipleship from Sydney Carter's "Lord of the Dance." When she preached to the class, her sermon met with very different responses. Some students applauded her combination of very different images of cross-bearing and joyous movement to music into the concept of discipleship. Others reacted negatively to the mental image of dancing with Christ. They suggested that the idea of the woman following the lead of a male Jesus (described elsewhere as "our intimate partner") violated the preacher's feminist commitments.

A final example shows still another way in which women preachers refashion metaphors. In the conclusion of her sermon on Romans 8:14-17, a woman wanted to enable listeners to claim confidently the gift of a relationship with God. The chief metaphor was "womb":

. . . It is in the freedom of surrender that God can enfold us and draw us near. We are safe in the dark womb of love—in the care of the Spirit, in the arms of Jesus. We can see in the warm darkness. We are not blinded by the Light. It is in our darkness that our spirit can see, can know, that we are the children of God.

This use of imagery made me uncomfortable in a way that "the Flood" and "the dance of discipleship" did not. First, there was the troubling mix of metaphors and epithets; Light, presented as a name, is a self-designation of Jesus. How can the Light that is absent in the womb simultaneously be the arms that embrace us? Second, other uses of this powerful metaphor impinge on our consideration of this preacher's ideas: psychological jargon (the longing to return to the womb); Jesus' conversation with Nicodemus ("How can a man be born when he is old? Can he enter a second time into his mother's womb and be born?"); Paul's descriptions of Christian maturity/perfection as the goal of every disciple (Phil. 3). In other words, other uses of the womb as metaphor make more powerful claims on the listener than the image presented by the preacher, and she depletes what evocative power it does have by mixing metaphors.

In order for new imagery (or usage) to take hold with integrity and staying power, it must be intelligible to the community in which it is spoken, and it also must read correctly the metaphor it seeks to replace. Women preachers should beware of universalizing women's experience just as men in the pulpit ought to reexamine the male-oriented, hierarchical language they may be using. Instead of gender-oriented images, new language drawn from a reference point in popular culture (such as "dance") is likely to be understood by the largest percentage of listeners. The metaphors should also be selected for their power to connect with the corporate memory of the community of faith. Such words not only generate shared agreement about meaning, they also evoke new awareness of the One who is beyond our ability to name.

"INTUITIVE" VERSUS "DIRECTIVE" COMMUNICATION

The tendency of women to use what I call "intuitive communication" is related both to their use of metaphor and to stereotypical "feminine syntax," discussed in the third section of this chapter. By "intuitive," I mean that women place higher reliance than men on meanings already shared between preacher and listeners to communicate their ideas. In this communication style, fresh metaphors have evocative power because of a frame of reference held in common. For example, when my parents are passengers in my car and giving directions, my mother is likely to say, "you know to turn up there, don't you?" while my father is more apt to say, "remember to turn left at the light." Both speakers intend to give the driver necessary information, but to the outsider, the woman's instructions are enigmatic. When men convey ideas, as in the pulpit, their words tend to have a higher information content.[25] This does not make men's communication better and more interesting; on the contrary, the result can be dull and pedantic. In general, however, male students in preaching class rely less on shared experience and more on "correct" terminology for presenting their message.

The intuitive nature of some women's sermons may be a conscious reflection of what they believe preaching is—and what it is not. Persuasion to a particular point of view and/or transmission of religious truths are not the goals of the preacher. Instead, preaching is a profound act of human connection and intimacy.[26] In order to *create* authentic intimacy, I believe, the woman preacher must lay the groundwork for the intuitive and/or nonverbal communication that will follow. "Faith connection" and "participation in the transforming power"[27] of the community are impossible if there is no one present to interpret the preacher's "unknown tongue."

A woman composing liturgical materials in worship class attempted to "create a mood" by inviting worshipers to contemplate particular sights and sounds. She offered this as the opening sentence for a Sunday morning service: "Gentle murmurs of raindrops on a tin roof stir our inner sense to a calming and peaceful inner spirit of worship."

The language was in itself soothing and peaceful—but there was nothing that directed the congregation's focus on worship rather than on a nap on a rainy Sunday morning. Nor did the opening sentence build or reinforce community. She could have retained her engaging imagery and still maintained the liturgical function of the opening sentence had her words been more directional: "The Spirit of Christ, like rain murmuring on a tin roof, gives calm and peace. That Spirit gently invites us now to join our hearts and voices in worshiping God."

Women's evocative language, rich with adjectives and adverbs, is opaque or turgid if it is missing the directive element that worshipers expect from a leader of worship. The preacher is not abusing ministerial power by using more instrumental or specific language in the pulpit. The community's solidarity will be built on shared frustration or boredom if, lacking a common frame of reference, the preacher denies them the means to organize the impressionistic images offered during the sermon.

A second example demonstrates the need for a way to "organize" information given by the preacher. A woman in preaching class gave a brief autobiographical narrative based on the nativity story in Luke 2. She began by describing a long-term project of hers: creating and painting figures for a nativity scene. As she worked on the project over the years, she said several things had happened: (1) the story kept changing; (2) she realized it was her story; (3) others hearing her talk about her story claimed their story, too. She also mentioned showing her nativity scene to patients in a nursing home. She smiled and looked earnestly at the congregation as she concluded. I assumed that by "her story," she meant that her point of identification with the text changed according to other circumstances in her life—but she never explicated in what manner this happened. Because she failed to do this, listeners were not given means to make a similar identification. The intimacy of the setting and her expressive nonverbal communication helped maintain listener interest, but other students had difficulty summarizing "what she was getting at" during discussion afterwards. They reacted positively to her affability in the pulpit, but did not experience or learn anything beyond that. The Gospel narrative was never identified as a story of peculiar importance for their faith.

One strength in the woman's presentation, which I noted for the class, was that her narrative moved in a comfortable, logical way; she went from an observation about the story itself to the story as it affected her, and then to how it affected others. The organization of "intuitive" communication greatly aids listeners in discerning the message's underlying meaning and putting metaphors in context, just as being advised, "you know to turn up there, don't you?" makes far more sense when spoken at the logical moment rather than five minutes earlier.

Another pitfall of highly intuitive communication is that the preacher may believe she is being more concrete and directive than her listeners perceive. Because the purpose is clear in her own mind, she may be unaware that the congregation does not "know the code." For example, in discussing homiletical method for her sermon based on Psalm 137:1-6, a woman preacher stated her aim was to end the sermon with a clear challenge having specificity and particularity: to claim our role in God's ongoing redemption, suggesting not just what we might do, but who we might be.[28] The preacher employed a song called "Zion's Song" as a refrain throughout the sermon: "Zion's songs are meant for Babylon." The illustrations, drawn from her experiences in Nairobi, traditional black preaching, and Holocaust Remembrance Day, were vivid and moving:

> I saw Kenyan women dance and sing in response to the essence of life itself. It seemed to me looking on that they sing to know who they are. When they sing they proclaim with their bodies, their voices, and their spirits, that their lives are rooted in a spiritual dimension that permeates their hard labors and their most oppressive situations.[29]

While the illustrations were memorable in their own right, they did not disclose what the preacher or the psalm-writer meant by "Zion's songs," other than songs sung to God, which also function to reinforce communal identity. Nor did the sermon reveal what the preacher understood as God's ongoing redemption in which humans may have a part. The message was not controversial so much as elusive; it created a mood rather than communicating content or enabling response to the Word proclaimed.

Is this a call for a moratorium on the intuitive and nonverbal aspects of any communication? Should we assume that the only frame of reference shared by preacher and congregation is the worship context itself? That isn't my intention. I do want to exhort women preachers to become deliberate about balancing nonspecific imagery with ideas and principles to order and understand experiential language. Poetic, evocative imagery is regarded as stereotypical of feminine communication in our culture. Women in ministry are still considered a novelty: exceptions and, to some extent, a departure from what is normative. If the woman in the pulpit wants her message to get a fair hearing, she will refrain from reinforcing stereotypes and proclaim the Word using vocabulary that includes linear thinkers and nonpoets. In this way, she may indeed "enable a quality of faith connection" in which more intuitive, metaphorical communication is possible.

WOMEN'S SYNTAX AND
THE QUESTION OF AUTHORITY

The speech patterns dealt with in this section are necessarily limited to English-language preachers in North American culture. It must also be acknowledged that some of the characteristics described in the pages that follow are shared by male students in my preaching classes. However, while men largely abandon these patterns as they become more experienced in the pulpit, women preachers tend to maintain them. I believe their usage is related to power and cultural stereotypes as well as to gender: communication strategies of the less-powerful to the more-powerful. Men receive more positive reinforcement for claiming and speaking with authority in our culture. As a woman newscaster once commented, "There's still some subtle stereotyping done on women. A man gets angry, but a woman throws a tantrum. A man is strong, but a woman is bitchy."[30] Because seeing women in the pulpit and in other positions of "power" is still a novelty in our culture, it is possible that women preachers instinctively maintain language patterns that minimize anticipated resistance and reinforce cultural expectations regarding femininity.

In "Women in the Pulpit: Some Sociolinguistic Questions," Catherine Ziel identifies three syntactical patterns found more commonly in women's speech than men's: (1) relational or social language; (2) tag questions; and (3) adverbs and other qualifiers. I tested her assertions about syntax in two ways; first, I conducted a written survey of women in my preaching class, asking them to identify anything they thought was distinctive about the way women use language in preaching. I also listened to women's sermons for evidence of these speech patterns. Though the students interviewed tended to describe the difference in language use in terms of inclusiveness and noninclusiveness, some of their responses bear out Ziel's assertions.

First, women's predilection toward relational or social language: where men tend to speak of the world as something to be manipulated, and to place themselves at the center of actions that they describe, women are more likely to speak of other people and be less involved in the event to which they refer.[31] One student put it in a slightly different way: that women's illustrations and images are usually people- and relationship-oriented; men frequently use "power" images, institution images, and sports metaphors.[32] The opening paragraph of this sermon demonstrates both the tendency to speak of other people and to stay away from "power" images:

> As we find ourselves in the beginning of the season of Lent, we notice that somehow the Christian life is making a shift where the memories of yesterday move to the hopes of tomorrow. From Epiphany, which brings the news of the birth of Christ to the Gentiles and which marks the beginning of Jesus' ministry, we are making this quantum leap to the passion and death of Christ.[33]

The preacher is neither the center nor the initiator of action in these sentences. Instead, she stands with the congregation in *observing* what "the Christian life" is doing, clearly not directing the action of the text of her listeners.

In a similar manner, another student preacher identified herself with the congregation in the opening sentences of the sermon, placing them as objects rather than subjects of action:

> I wonder if you all have been disturbed by the news lately. It seems as though most of the news broadcasts are full of people wanting to hurt other people. The attacks in the Persian Gulf are a good example.[34]

THEOLOGY IN METAPHOR AND GRAMMAR

In reviewing sermon tapes and manuscripts, I did not discover the element of "less involvement in an event" noted by others analyzing women's communication. Instead, introductions to sermons were characterized more by stories told in the first-person, usually inviting the congregation to identify with something the preacher observed or experienced. The difference between this communication pattern and that of male students is that men's autobiographical stories depend on action they took, or an analogy between their particular experience and the lesson derived from the text.

The tendency toward relational and social language lends strength in women's preaching. It invites listeners to consider a situation or idea together rather than putting the spotlight on the preacher herself. The prevalence of plural pronouns suggests solidarity with the congregation, helping them bridge the distance of hearing a "strange" voice from the pulpit. Though it doesn't immediately claim the same authority as a male preacher's first-person parabolic narrative, it does not undermine the woman preacher's credibility, either.

The use of "tag questions" is also regarded as a second characteristic of feminine speech. These sentences begin as declaratives but end with questions: "It was good, wasn't it?" Because they are characteristic of oral rather than written communication, sermon manuscripts by women do not often demonstrate the first form of tag question. When tags do occur, they are more likely to be found in the opening paragraphs of the message, as a means of inviting the congregation to consider the subject of the day's text:

> The gospel today is filled with questions. It begins with questions by the disciples: "Rabbi, who sinned, this man or his parents, that he was born blind?" . . . Children ask a lot of questions, don't they? "Why is rain wet?" "Why is grass green?" Probably you asked your parents like that, or you have tried to answer questions like that from your children.[35]

Tag questions can occur as disguised or weak imperatives in the liturgy: "Shall we pray together?" as opposed to the "Let us pray'' used more often by male clergy. In preaching, women use tags in the form of rhetorical questions, inviting the congregation to think about something rather than to give assent:

> Have you ever thought about what it would actually be like to stand on water? I bet taking that first step out of the boat was downright frightening. . . . Can you picture Jesus as he looked into Peter's eyes as he spoke to him? How would *you* feel having Jesus look into your eyes, saying, ''I have prayed for you . . .''?[36]

Women's use of tag questions in preaching is an asset if they are appropriate to the subject matter and the stage of the sermon where they occur. A confession of faith or announcement of good news should not be couched in terms of tag questions. In the early portions of a message, women's tag questions may engage the listeners and refrain from limiting their possible ''answers'' prematurely. Near the end of the sermon, however, a tag question is more likely to be perceived as uncertainty on the preacher's part, undermining the authority listeners subconsciously expect to be communicated in a conclusion. The intonation with which a tag question is asked may communicate whether it is being posed from a position of weakness or strength. A falling intonation at the end of the question may be heard as threatening or sarcastic: ''We've never been Prodigal Sons or Daughters, have we?'' In addition to this, the use of tag questions in everyday conversation by both women and men may vary from one part of the country to another.

The third characteristic of women's speech patterns, frequent use of adverbs, qualifying words and phrases, is commonplace in sermons by women preachers. Ziel says that qualifiers leave ideas open-ended, allowing listeners the freedom to draw their own conclusions. However, they cannot communicate the same competence or authority as straightforward, unambiguous asser- tions. (No congregation wants its preacher to ''suggest'' there are ''approximately'' four Gospels!) Overuse of qualifiers makes a woman sound uncertain about the facts, redundant, or lacking in confidence. In the sermon on John 9:1-38 quoted a few paragraphs earlier, the preacher went on to say, ''We try to answer questions, and we do a *pretty* good job *sometimes*'' [emphasis mine]. The lasting impression made by such a sentence is that the preacher is whistling in the dark. Another example of qualifiers undermining the credibility of the ideas being presented is shown in this excerpt from a sermon on the doctrine of "assurance":

> The letter to the Galatians describes the fruit[s] of the spirit as "love, joy, peace, patience, gentleness and goodness." Those *would seem to be* characteristics that we *could* identify in ourselves and in others. And to be known by one's fruit *would seem to mean* to be recognized by what one does. . . . [emphasis mine]

It is ironic that by refraining from indicative action verbs (These *are* characteristics that we *identify* . . .) the preacher inadvertently lacks assurance in her syntax. Other preachers employ modifiers for a calculated purpose in their sermons. The qualifiers "so, very, really, kind of, such," rather than adding emphasis, have the cumulative effect of diminishing the strength of ideas being communicated:

> It sounds so simple—and yet so unbelievable. When I was a child, it was so easy to believe that Jesus was my Savior. Ours was the "Romans" road. Ours the simple faith. As I grew, the world grew more difficult to understand and the simple answer did not satisfy. Suffering in the world. Problems in the church. . . .[17]

In this quotation, the repeated use of "so" was deliberate. It negated the simplicity being described. The result was an increased sense of the preacher's authority among listeners. She communicated an understanding of the complex world in which they lived, and the questions that challenged their faith as well as her own.

Some women preachers who speak from notes rather than manuscript are prone to use another sort of modifier. In the example below, qualifiers function as "filler." They give the preacher time to recall her next idea, but do not convince the listener of the credibility of the preacher or her message:

> This story is found only in Luke and is told in typical Lukan fashion. Zacchaeus was not your ordinary typical person of that day. Zacchaeus was small in stature, height-wise.

While male student preachers use "y'know" or "um" or shift their weight from one foot to the other to give themselves time,

137

women in the pulpit use modifiers to explain things that are self-evident, such as "small in stature, height-wise." Unfortunately, the tendency to use "fillers" is not confined to the pulpit; when this syntactical problem exists, it is manifested in all oral communication. It poses a greater hazard for women than men in ministry because women are expected to *establish* credibility rather than simply maintain it.

IMPLICATIONS FOR WOMEN'S LANGUAGE IN PREACHING

Evaluative comments have already been made about particular aspects of women's choice of words in the pulpit, such as inclusive versus noninclusive language. If a woman preacher accepts the underlying assumption that certain words and structures are *heard* as gender-related in our culture (regardless of what she intended in using them), by what guidelines does she discern the communication pattern that fits herself, the listeners, the content of her message, and the context in which it is said?

One homiletician suggests developing an "androgynous" style: the capacity to adapt to varying communication situations so that the strengths associated with both genders can be used.[38] This style focuses on the sermon content more directly than on the speaker, context, and listeners. If, for example, the sermon is based on one of Jesus' pronouncements, the preacher's syntax will be consciously more authoritative than if she is preaching on a miracle story (from the perspective of a beneficiary of or witness to the event). In the latter situation, the preacher will communicate wonder, joy, or a confession of faith, conveyed through what our culture regards as feminine speech patterns.

The androgynous style is effective in expository preaching, if there is already some equilibrium in the preacher-congregation relationship. Other guidelines are needed for those cases where (1) sermon content does not suggest the obvious method for proclamation; (2) the woman preacher and congregation do not know each other; and (3) the larger question of language and the liturgy is considered. Additional observations that give more attention to the interactive nature of worship may help the woman preacher make better-informed decisions about language.

First, a congregation incorporates new metaphors more readily than it replaces old ones, especially if the preacher gives them a frame of reference for understanding the language she introduces. Introducing biblical and "new" images and metaphors for the divine, or demythologizing old imagery, is likely to be understood by listeners and may facilitate a deeper knowledge and awareness of God. The preacher will meet congregational resistance and incomprehension if she alters or deletes well-known liturgical materials whose evocative power lies, in part, with the language left intact. Any pastor who has read a modern paraphrase of the 23rd Psalm at a funeral, or who tries unsuccessfully to lead the congregation in praying, "Our Father and Mother, who art in heaven. . . . " is aware of the iconic function of the more familiar forms. Symbolic words without obvious referents and controversial changes in language should be introduced and discussed in church school or another forum.

Second, a woman preaching to a congregation for the first time should tailor her material to rely less on the intuitive level of communication and more on the informational/instrumental. A congregation has to learn how to listen to any new preacher—male or female—and in their first worship service together, a wise preacher will not assume the degree of familiarity essential for effective intuitive interaction. Successful communication in her subsequent sermons depends on the cultivation of the preacher-congregation relationship as a "de-coder" and the effectiveness of the preacher's nonverbal communication.

Finally, congregational response to long-term "feminine syntax" from a woman preacher may be difficult for the listeners themselves to identify. It may manifest itself in the degree of comfort or discomfort they feel in more relationship-oriented communication. The preacher may experience it as ongoing internal misgivings about her own authority and credibility. If the listeners consistently remember more about the preacher or how they felt during the sermon than what was said, this may indicate the need to alter language patterns and incorporate the communication gifts associated with both genders.

I believe there is truth to the feminist claim that the distinctions between sermon, song, action, and prayer *may* be blurred when a woman is leading worship. . . . This can be attributed to women's spirituality, which brings into question centuries-old patterns of worship as a woman embodies a message rather than simply delivering it.

*C*ut off from their history in patriarchal worship, ritual acts and symbols mean whatever the liturgist or community has in mind. There need not be discussion or consensus on the meaning; a symbol may be entirely without referents, if it is nonetheless evocative.

*P*reaching and liturgy should communicate that one's identity in the community that meets Sunday morning is based on one's faith commitment—not on sex, race, or insider's knowledge. The immanence of God should not be celebrated at the expense of divine transcendence that is present for other people in other places and times.

SEVEN

WOMEN PREACHERS AND LITURGY

The church is experiencing a period of renewed interest in the relationship of preaching to liturgy, accelerated, though not inaugurated by the sweeping reforms of the Second Vatican Council. The evolution of contemporary feminism, beginning with the foundation of the National Organization for Women (in the same decade as Vatican II) is also making its mark on worship patterns in the western church.

It is not my purpose to give a catalogue of feminist liturgies, nor to prescribe a single paradigm for women leading worship. My primary interests are: (1) what women pastors of various traditions are doing in the local church on Sunday morning; (2) the extent to which women's liturgical patterns incorporate new acts without abandoning old structures and meanings; and (3) the extent to which women replace traditional ritual acts or invest them with new meanings. The relationship of these other liturgical acts to the sermon is an ongoing emphasis. Therefore, less attention is given to ritual acts developed and/or led by women in which preaching does not occur, such as the "naming and baptism" celebration in Rosemary Radford Ruether's *Women-Church*. Liturgies by and for women outside the Christian tradition, as well as liturgies composed for private gatherings or occasions, are also beyond the scope of this chapter. "Women's Freedom Litany" used at a weekly Mother Goddess ritual and published in *WomanSpirit* and anthologies of liturgical materials, such as *Festivals,* are interesting in their own right, but because their presentation is not integrated with the act of preaching, they are omitted from lengthy discussion here.

Some feminists make the claim that when women preach, the line between sermon, song, action, and prayer gets blurred. This is due in part to women's spirituality, which is not pulpit-centered but experiments with various media to embody the faith, reflecting women's diverse backgrounds in education, music, art, and service occupations.[1] If this is correct, it would follow that in worship led by women, the relationship of preaching to liturgy would resist analysis because of the difficulty in discerning where one ends and the other begins.

I believe there is truth to the feminist claim that the distinctions between sermon, song, action, and prayer *may* be blurred when a woman is leading worship. The majority of clergywomen in the United States, however, follow one of four or five mainstream liturgical patterns. These patterns manifest different understandings of the place of the proclaimed word in Sunday morning worship. A brief overview of these patterns, with examples from women's liturgical leadership, where feasible, leads me to conclude: (1) women whose leadership of worship "fits" one of the mainstream patterns exhibit a remarkable diversity in theological orientation; (2) "blurred lines" worship often reflects a liberation feminist perspective (as opposed to the diversity of perspectives manifested in more traditional patterns). In presenting the patterns with which most clergywomen work, particular attention is given to the ways women's theological diversity is manifested, and the relationship suggested between the sermon and other acts of worship.

WOMEN AND MAINSTREAM LITURGICAL PATTERNS

The first pattern of worship under consideration is the Roman Catholic service of word and table (Mass). This liturgical pattern has unchanging parts ("ordinary") and parts that vary ("propers") according to the lessons, the season of the church year, and the person leading the service. It is not possible to present an example of the way women pastors maintain the status quo, incorporate new ritual acts or meanings into old structures, or replace old liturgical acts with new ones; women are not ordained in this tradition and therefore do not have the authority to make such decisions.

Women may, however, be *invited* to make suggestions about worship, providing they do not deviate from *The Constitution on the Sacred Liturgy*. One such instance of this, which was later published, is the Mass of Freedom for Women. It was a one-time occasion in a local church, rather than ongoing change in the service.[2] It conformed to the prescribed pattern for the liturgy of the word: three lessons, a "psalm" response, and a homily. The Gospel reading, Luke 18:1-5 (the woman and the unjust judge) was supplemented by readings from Sojourner Truth and Catherine of Siena. Though a transcript of the homily (preached by a nun) was not provided, the underlying theme for the Mass is suggested by the prayer before the liturgy of the word:

> A prophet is never without honor, except in her own country. Let's take "prophet" in the sense of one who speaks for another and pray that we may remain mindful of what we say to one another because of our own different social involvements. We bear witness to, and for, one another, and so become a people who care for one another. We ask this through Christ our Lord. So be it.[3]

The invocation's structure and content both reflect the struggles of its composer. The prayer does not follow traditional collect form even though it serves the appointed function of introducing the readings. The content of the prayer is like the "cropped" Gospel reading in that both are in service to the theme: women's struggle for freedom and justice. In summary, the writers of this liturgy were successful in articulating a feminist agenda within the limitations of this worship pattern. However, since the liturgy was a one-time event for a special occasion, it cannot be considered in the same light as the work of women who lead a community of faith in its worship on an ongoing basis.

The second pattern found in mainstream western Christianity is a balance between word and table in Protestant worship. A variety of factors contributed to its development: the desire to return to Scripture in liturgical materials, interest in the worship life of the early church, recovery of the missionary character of the whole church, ecumenism, and the desire for more participatory worship.[4] The sermon normally comes before the Lord's Supper, and there is more latitude for individual expression and innovation in the liturgy of the word. Depending on her denomination, the woman leading worship may have the liberty to supplement readings from the Bible with noncanonical materials. Prayers may be extemporaneous or part of her church's written tradition. She may preach on one of the texts, give a topical sermon, or focus on the season of the church year in her message. Only the words of institution in the eucharistic prayer are an unchanging part of the liturgy.

An extemporaneous prayer by a woman preacher during the liturgy of the word manifests thematic unity between the sermon, which was on the blood of Christ, and the Eucharist that followed:

O, that your light, your truth, your blood may be poured out on this body of believers in the purity of your love. And may it be received by the same love that raised Jesus Christ from the dead. Amen.[5]

The preacher is intentional in leading the congregation to consider word and table as two parts of an integrated whole. The language used is traditional, inclusive, and familiar to most in the congregation. The prayer is not explicitly an invocation, which one might expect before the sermon. Instead, the content foreshadows the goal of the sermon: to encourage a quality and degree of interpersonal intimacy made possible by Christ's sacrificial love, here symbolized by blood. The theological orientation of this woman stands in contrast to the composer of the Roman Catholic order of service. In the Mass of Freedom for Women, feminist theology is on the agenda, where the extemporaneous prayer of a Protestant clergywoman shows a more traditional understanding of corporate worship.

A second example from a Protestant service is the closing worship celebration of a National Clergywomen's Consultation of The United Methodist Church. While this service of word and table was not a Sunday morning service, it is included because Sharon Brown Christopher and Leontine T. C. Kelly, who wrote the liturgy, meant it to be a model for those attending to take back to their local churches. The sermon, "Make Plain the Vision," was drawn from these scriptures read during worship: Habakkuk 2:1-4, Revelation 21:1, 3-7, and Luke 4:16-21. It should be noted that this combination of readings does not occur in the *Common Lectionary,* and each reading is "cropped" from a longer pericope suggested in the lectionary. The opening sentences, Isaiah 43:19-21, serve the theme of God's vision for the future. The prayer of confession, while continuing the theme of vision, is interesting both for its use of metaphor and theological orientation:

> O God, you are like a Weaverwoman in our lives. Out of the energy of the universe you have spun each one of us. . . . We admit that our own choices have severed us from your loom of life and created rents in the whole of our human fabric. . . . We have often refused to ask the hard questions that need to be asked for the sake of the well-being of all people. . . . The ache of scars from previous hurts and risks has inhibited us from daring to embody and proclaim your love and justice. O Weaverwoman God, open our eyes to the mystery and power of your Spirit. Refresh us with the light of your vision. . . . Reattach us to your loom. . . . In the name of Christ, the One who was at one with all of life. Amen.[6]

The extended metaphors about weaving may function as effective symbols in a congregation that already knows and values the metaphor, as this group of worshipers did. The prayer of confession discloses not only a feminist orientation (addressing God as "Weaverwoman") but other theological issues at stake for the community. Interpersonal and intrapersonal failure are confessed, but not offenses against God per se. Naming Christ as "the One who was at one with all of life" suggests, but does not prove, a lower Christology than was inherent in the invocation about the blood of Christ mentioned earlier. The Spirit is mentioned, but the writers' trinitarian theology is not clear. Overall, the primary image of God presented is a deity who resembles the worshipers in some sense. The divine-human relationship in the liturgy of the word is that of cooperative partners revealing and fulfilling a shared vision.

The third liturgical pattern predominant in western Protestant churches is the "preaching service" in which the sermon is the longest and focal point in Sunday morning worship. It traces its roots to worship in the synagogue and the synaxis portion of early Christian worship. Its form at present ranges from a completely fluid, spontaneous "warm-up act" before the sermon, to a fixed sequence of ritual acts and words with differing histories and functions. Though we may think of worship during the first centuries of the church as less structured than what Christians today do on Sunday morning, lectionaries and written prayers for the day, time, and season of the church year were used quite early in the development of corporate worship.

The "word as center" pattern of worship can actually be subdivided into two: worship in which the sermon, often based on a lectionary text for the day, employs other liturgical materials that complement the theme/text, and worship in which there is no integrating principle or theme manifested.

Women have left their mark on this pattern of worship, too. The feminist movement was one impetus for the development of the National Council of Churches' *Inclusive Language Lectionary,* an attempt to "recast the language of scripture so that it addresses women and men equally." This publication gives the texts for each Sunday, but does not offer supporting material for presenting a unified theme for worship. One resource that does meet this need is Janet Morley's *All Desires Known.* Using the lectionary of the Church of England's *Alternative Service Book* (1980), original collects for each Sunday of the year help tie the service together. The collect for Christmas 2 (Luke 2:41-52) reads:

> God of community, whose call is more insistent than ties of family or blood; may we so respect and love those whose lives are linked with ours that we fail not in loyalty to you, but make choices according to your will, through Jesus Christ, amen.[7]

The lack of gender-specific names for God suggests that the woman who wrote the prayer is a feminist. Other aspects of the prayer hint at the woman's comfort with a traditional theology of worship: her adherence to traditional collect form, her understanding of the authority of the divine will in her life, and her concern for thematic unity based on the Gospel reading for the day. It does not use strikingly feminine language, though the collect for Lent 4, which is Mothering Sunday (Isaiah 46:3-4; 49:14-16; 66:7-13; Hosea 11:1-4), does so on the basis of what appears in the texts:

> God our mother, you hold our life within you; nourish us at your breast, and teach us to walk alone. Help us so to receive your tenderness and respond to your challenge that others may draw life from us, in your name, amen.[8]

Another example, which combines fidelity to the *Common Lectionary* with the creativity of the woman leading worship, featured a sermon on Mary and Martha and developed the idea of needing to take time to be with God and hear God's voice. The texts used in the service were Luke 19:38-41, Colossians 1:21-29, and Psalm 139:13-18. The two hymns used were traditional, without changing language to make them more inclusive: "Praise to the Lord, the Almighty" and "Take Time to Be Holy." The unison prayer of confession was composed by the preacher for the theme of the day:

> God of stillness, God of action, we confess that we have yet to find a proper balance to our lives. We need you to teach us how to find the time and space for praying and learning and for doing our share of serving as we offer our skills and abilities. In work and in prayer may you enable us to be worthy disciples of Jesus, the Word of your love, amen.[9]

This example is included because the woman preacher wrote the prayer and chose the second hymn on what proved to be the point of the sermon, rather than on the lectionary texts alone. The focus of the prayer is on the lessons to be learned from Jesus' words to Martha, not on Mary and Martha as women. In the last two prayers, then, we see that a feminist commitment can find liturgical expression both in using feminine imagery and in preaching on narrative texts involving women. The women who composed the prayers were skillful at balancing traditional metaphors with less familiar ones. There is also a balance of attention between interpersonal and divine-human relationships.

The language engages rather than startles worshipers. The last prayer is more clearly Christian than the one before it. All three prayers effectively integrate text, sermon, and other materials in a familiar worship pattern.

The other worship pattern in which proclamation is the center is that in which there isn't a clear connection between the sermon and other acts of worship. This liturgical structure is not the property of one gender or denomination, but because women have inherited and perpetuated it, further discussion of it is appropriate. The materials used for the "hymn sandwich" may be selected from published works or be the woman preacher's own composition. The order and content of the service may reflect a long congregational tradition or the idiosyncrasies of the woman leading worship. This is not to say such worship lacks integrity; what is missing is unity.

In this pattern of worship, the prayer before the sermon may be required to carry more freight than an invocation normally does. For example, one woman preaching on Matthew 13:24-30 (the parable of the wheat and tares) began with this extemporaneous prayer:

> Our heavenly Father, as we come to you this morning with bowed hearts, open our minds that we can hear what you have for us. This is a beautiful day and we give you thanks for it. And as the day progresses, we pray that our minds will take in what you have laid out for us and whatsoever it is, we ask your guidance in everything. In his name, amen.

This is not a controversial invocation that will horrify, thrill, or infuriate the congregation. The preacher addressed God as "heavenly Father," but otherwise there does not appear to be a feminist or anti-feminist bias. What is the problem? The prayer doesn't "belong" to the sermon, nor to any other portion of the service. It expresses reverence, but cannot be identified positively as Christian. As such, it will not lead worshipers into the next part of the service, nor aid them in focusing on the sermon theme.

Sometimes the lack of unity between sermon and the rest of worship is manifested not by the liturgical acts themselves but by the preacher's leadership style. The type of interaction with the congregation is incongruous with the words being said. For example, a responsive call to worship printed in the bulletin suggests one degree of formality in the service, particularly when "King James" English is used. At one service I attended, the words to the call to worship were liturgically sympathetic with the sermon topic, but in calling the congregation to stand for the beginning of worship, the woman pastor said:

> Good morning! Isn't it wonderful to be here today? Amen? AMEN! In a moment we're all going to stand together for the call to worship, which you'll find printed on the first page of your bulletin. The call to worship helps bring us together in our purpose for being here: to praise God and enjoy our unity and fellowship in Christ. It is a call to celebration and joy, because of God's love for us and our love for one another. So let's now stand and read it together.

A layman read a lesson from Deuteronomy, and his staid manner contrasted so sharply with the preacher's during the call to worship that the congregation's attention was on the differences in leadership styles rather than the actual words being said. The masculine voice called for "obedience to God's word" but allowed listeners to remain passive. The feminine voice demanded a high degree of involvement, emotional and spiritual as well as physical. It should be noted, parenthetically, that the preface to the call to worship was not used as a substitute for an informal time of sharing congregational prayer concerns later in the hour; that is, the "mood" of worship changed abruptly several times during the service, with no apparent reason except gender difference.

The final pattern in mainstream western Christianity is one shared by a number of groups: many Pentecostal churches, charismatic denominations, some black churches, "deliverance" sects and other traditions in which invitations to conversion or recommitment or other activities regularly occur in the course of worship. In this noneucharistic, usually Protestant, order of worship the sermon is considered important, but it also functions as a catalyst or prelude to a second focal point in the liturgy that follows it. Proclamation by one person leads to individual and/or congregational acts of devotion, which are seen as voluntary, Spirit-enabled responses to preaching or, more strongly, as the result of it.

This liturgical pattern presents something of a paradox where women preachers are concerned. On the one hand, the groups with this style of worship have been open to the leadership of women longer than many mainline denominations, so we would expect an abundance of material by women. On the other hand, it is difficult to produce written examples from this liturgical pattern because spontaneity is valued as a sign that the sermon is "working on" those at worship by the Holy Spirit. One of the women preachers from this tradition, however, wrote an account of "A Typical Weekend in Angelus Temple" (Foursquare Gospel Temple) and described her order of worship and congregational participation. Her description included the following:

> Flanking Sister McPherson, the evangelist, and filling the entire platform, are grouped the aged veterans of the Civil War, smiling, nodding, singing, encouraging. The revival is on. Song after song is lifted heavenward and supported by the strains of the great Angelus Temple organ. . . . An aged minister is praying now. Heads bowed everywhere. Fervent amens from every quarter of the building. Now, we are preaching the Word. . . . We read to them the Word of the Lord, the old, old story that is ever new—the story of the rugged cross whereon the King of Glory died. . . . Rapidly we paint the scenes one by one. . . . The altar call is given. Eyes, blinded with tears, are groping their way into the aisles. . . . Tremulously, earnestly, with upstretched hands they are singing, "I've wasted many precious years, Now I'm coming home. . . ." We find our own eyes brimming with happy tears as we watch our congregation filing out through the doors into the kindly afternoon sunshine.[10]

Gender issues are more subtle in such accounts; it is only after reading descriptions of a number of evangelistic meetings that the follow recurrent characteristics become plain: (1) McPherson rarely mentioned the presence of another woman on the platform; (2) the men described in her reports were all avid supporters, flanking her on all sides, or converts/recipients of healing, moved to tears. The language and style of "A Typical Weekend" is also typical of her sermons: gushing, emotional, and traditionally Pentecostal in theology. McPherson's modern counterparts might be Frances Hunter, Jill Briscoe, and other women free-lance evangelists with a relatively small, but intensely loyal following.

A second example of a "word as catalyst" liturgical pattern that is popular particularly (though not solely) among women in traditions that do not ordain women, is the Agape Meal or love feast. They have discovered that this ritual meal can be invested with various symbolic meanings reflecting different theological orientations. It is both structured and spontaneous, in that celebration of a love feast is planned in advance, but the words spoken during the liturgy vary from one occasion to another. Sometimes the meal is called by another name. Its placement following a liturgy of the word, the simplicity of the food shared, and the extemporaneous "testimonies" that may occur during the meal are what identify it as an Agape Meal. Some traditions (such as the United Methodists) publish orders of service for the Agape Meal; when the person leading worship uses published resources, the element of personal creativity is lessened. At a love feast conducted by a seminary women's center, worship began by singing the following song by Miriam Therese Winter:

Mother and God, to You we sing:
wide is Your womb, warm is Your wing.
In you we live, move, and are fed,
sweet, flowing milk, life-giving bread.
Mother and God, to You we bring
all broken hearts, all broken wings.[11]

After readings from Scripture (but no homily) they commenced the love feast by using "Blessing the Bread: A Litany"

In the beginning was God
In the beginning
the source of all that is
In the beginning
God yearning
God moaning
God laboring

THE WOMAN IN THE PULPIT

God giving birth
God rejoicing . . .[12]

The focus in this Agape Meal was on building a sense of sisterhood among the women present, and familiarizing the new women students with feminine metaphors for God. Participants took turns literally feeding each other after the bread and juice were distributed. The litany for blessing the bread generated anticipation of what Mother God and women united could accomplish together. (To make sure the point was made, the liturgy was preceded by a lengthy game of "women's issues bingo"!)

The worship experiences described in these four patterns share several characteristics: first, they usually occurred in Sunday morning worship. Scripture was read and, with the exception of the last example, preaching of some sort occurred. The Bible was understood as divine revelation and held to be authoritative in some sense, though the hermeneutical starting points were not uniform.

Second, the women quoted represent a wide range of theological and liturgical orientations, from very conservative to liberation feminists, and from high church to low. A service in the Angelus Temple and a 1983 Clergywomen's Consultation reflect very different understandings of soteriology, ecclesiology, and Christology. Yet in their diversity, they nonetheless concur in the assumption that the primary activity in worship is interaction between God and the community of faith. To borrow a phrase from Geoffrey Wainwright, [their] worship is a faithful human response to the revelation of God's being, character, beneficence, and will.[13] A change is effected in worshipers by this divinely enabled response to God's self-disclosure.

Third, in all the examples noted, women leading worship utilized a basic structure of worship they inherited. They did not judge it so patriarchal, hierarchical, or otherwise oppressive to preclude it from being a vehicle of "faithful human response" to gracious divine initiative. This is not to say the authors of all the liturgical resources they used held this point of view, but the women preaching and leading worship chose to incorporate the material in a way reflecting this understanding.

A fourth observation: within the framework of these four or five patterns, it is easier to find examples of integration or nonintegration of preaching and liturgy in services where preaching is the center of worship than in word and table services. This may be because most traditions whose worship has the dual foci of word and table have been slower to ordain women, or still consider women unordainable. Churches whose tradition is word-centered tend to enforce less structure in the liturgy, and value the gifts and creativity of the individual preacher—thus being a more ready vehicle of expression for women leading worship.

LIBERATION FEMINIST LITURGIES: FIVE CHARACTERISTICS

At the beginning of the chapter, I noted a feminist theory that distinctions between sermon, song, action, and prayer are blurred when women lead worship. This can be attributed to women's spirituality, which brings into question centuries-old patterns of worship as a woman embodies a message rather than simply delivering it. Despite this claim, a substantial number of women clergy, for whatever reasons, have chosen to maintain in large part the liturgical structures they inherited. Even when a woman in my preaching class decided to conclude her sermon on Luke 10:25-37 by saying, "In the name of the Mother, the Son, and the Holy Spirit, amen," she adhered to the custom of ending a homily with a trinitarian formula that was distinct from the message itself. Though her choice of language indicates a feminist agenda, this feminism did not lead her to adopt a new mode of proclaiming or "embodying" her sermon.

I maintain, then, that although women's spirituality *may* result in forms of worship that do not correspond to the patterns described earlier, these resultant forms are not typical of all women who lead worship. If Jacquelyn Grant's taxonomy were employed here, we might say that "blurred lines" are more likely to be the creation of liberation feminists and rejectionists—female or male—than by women preachers as a whole. Women's spirituality is one contributing factor to feminist ways of worship; alienation from the

153

institutional church, a shift in the loci of authority, and, occasionally, lack of knowledge about the history of Christian worship and theology are others. The result is that the worship materials they publish, in which boundaries between sermons, song, and prayer are blurred, are more suitable for in-house, occasional services than for Sunday morning in the local church. Rather than using four or five *patterns* of liturgical structure that demonstrate relationships between proclamation and liturgy, the liberation feminist or rejectionist manifests five *characteristics* that pertain to the content more than to the form of worship.

First, a sense of alienation from mainstream worship (often used as a synonym for church) is an underlying theme in these feminist liturgies. The feeling of no longer belonging and the accompanying hermeneutic of suspicion impel the feminist to experiment freely with liturgical forms, and just as freely to discard them after experimentation. One prominent United Methodist clergywoman writes of the misogyny feminists perceive in dominant liturgical patterns:

> Some women [clergy] are withdrawing or leaving the church. They are choosing not to participate in a church that abuses them, denies their experience, devalues them, affirms the unholy, makes them sick. For the women who must leave, it is a moment of standing upright, saying yes to life, and moving on.[14]

In a similar vein, another feminist suggested that present institutional forms of liturgy feed on and encourage the passivity of women and the dominance of men in society. The oppressiveness of mainline liturgical patterns is more than a matter of masculine names and metaphors; it is a sacralization of patriarchal history in Scripture and tradition. It embraces imperial and hierarchical orderings of groups of people.[15] An example may help clarify the perceived oppressiveness: in old Ash Wednesday liturgies, ashes were imposed on a penitent's forehead with the words, "Remember, O man, that dust thou art, and to dust thou shalt return. Repent and believe the Gospel." A feminist critique of this liturgy would not be limited to addressing the penitent as "man," but might challenge the appropriateness of one person announcing the guilt of another, particularly as the penitent would be kneeling while the officiating clergy would be standing. Liberation and radical feminists explicitly reject hierarchical forms of liturgical leadership.[16]

The sermon, therefore, cannot be a monologue reinforcing dominance and submission by virtue of an elevated pulpit and/or sense of the preacher as one set apart for special and sacred work. To overcome alienating hierarchical tendencies, preaching must become relational and dialogical. The result is that the sermon is not always easy to distinguish from other moments in worship when many people may take turns speaking. It may resemble a small group discussion on a topic or text. It is understood as belonging to the community, in particular the community of women.[17]

And how does the sense of alienation find expression in feminist liturgies? One example is given by Rosemary Radford Ruether, who suggests that a newly forming covenant community recite the "Exorcism of the Powers and Principalities of Patriarchy," which often precedes baptism or baptismal renewal in *Women-Church*. One person holds a candle during the rite, another rings a bell at the conclusion of each exorcism statement:

—Powers of corruption of our humanity, which turn males into instruments of domination and shape women to be tools of submission, begone! . . .
—Powers of domestic violence, which assault children, women, and the weak and elderly in the home and hold them in bondage to fear and self-hatred, begone! . . .[18]

Ruether's work provides a curious contrast to liturgies produced by other feminists. Though the various symbols used in *Women-Church* are rarely explicated and provide much of the order and movement in their services, the spoken word is invested with greater power and significance than in Miriam Therese Winter's occasional services. The appeal of Ruether's liturgies is primarily cognitive; the symbols, often borrowed from Roman Catholic and Anglican tradition, are visual aids more than agents of transformation. Ironically, though Ruether's liturgies suggest that words are powerful agents of change, preaching is never mentioned as a function of ministers (or anyone else) in *Women-Church*. It is not precluded, either.

A second assumption that informs and shapes feminist worship is an emphasis on divine immanence rather than transcendence. Worshipers aspire not to reconciliation with God, but solidarity with the One whose will is their self-actualization and the attainment of a truly inclusive community. In some instances, distinctions between divine and human are eschewed or forgotten, so that it is difficult to determine when (or to whom) one is praying. The "blurring of boundaries" is particularly evident here; it is difficult to tell whether the following is a prayer to God, a pep-talk to oneself, or an exhortation to the congregation:

> Co-Author of Life Divine:
> May I cooperate with Your ideas for me. May the story You are able to write through me be one filled with spirit, one filled with compassion, one worthy of others' readings. . . . May I trust Your Co-Authorship and be able to see when I deviate too far from the story You would like my presence to tell.[19]

The writer of the prayer did not indicate its intended placement within a corporate worship service. The prayer echoes the liberation feminist rejection of hierarchical liturgical leadership by playing down the "hierarchical" nature of the divine-human relationship. The theology expressed is not trinitarian, and a reader may wonder where the Incarnate Christ figures in the faith of the person praying. The particularity of the Incarnation is often a point of contention in liberation feminist worship.

A second example of divine immanence and mutuality finding expression is in a credal statement by another feminist clergywoman:

> I believe that
> Where I stand at this particular moment
> Linked to my faith journey
> A perspective of seeing, being, and becoming
> I order and create with my Co-Creator . . .
> . . . I am woman.
> I am related to all of God's family.[20]

Once again, this material was offered outside the context of an order of service, but the closing lines suggest it was not intended for use on Sunday morning. The subject of the credal statement is primarily oneself and one's own experiences. This is in contrast to the earliest baptismal confessions of faith, which were as simple as "Jesus is Lord." It departs from the historical understanding of creeds being a corporate recital of God's saving acts.[21] For the person reciting this credal statement, mention of God's "saving acts" is limited to those experienced by the speaker. The focus on immanence does permit the speaker to look toward the future, and what God may do or reveal there, but it does not acknowledge God's transcendence of history that reaches into the past as well. This may be a side effect of a hermeneutic of suspicion that regards nearly all history as contaminated by patriarchy. One feminist liturgical scholar criticizes the ritualization of patriarchal memory in liturgy, but warns that without grounding in the particularity of historical events, which make liturgical celebration possible when connected with God's faithfulness, Christianity runs the risk of drifting off into Gnosticism.[22]

A third working assumption, which has been called something between ecumenicity and pluralism, is the idea that "we were women before we were Jews, Christians, or Moslems,"[23] so that sexuality becomes the most significant key to individual and group identity in worship. Theological and liturgical syncretism precludes consideration of a worship service as various components of a unified whole; the chief requirement of a liturgy is that it reflect the needs and aspirations of those participating, however disparate or conflicting their belief systems may be. With this as an operating assumption, paraliturgical acts are often elevated in significance. Cut off from their history in patriarchal worship, ritual acts and symbols mean whatever the liturgist or community has in mind. There need not be discussion or consensus on the meaning; a symbol may be entirely without referents, if it is nonetheless evocative.

Two examples from well-known producers of worship resources demonstrate this. First, in Rosemary Radford Ruether's "New Moon Ritual" for menstruating women, the setting calls for candles set up in a circle around a bowl in which a large candle floats on liquid. Crowns of flowers are placed on each woman's head.[24] Though one may recall the use of these symbols in Christian, Jewish, and/or Goddess worship, their *raison d'être* here is not given. What is given is that women participate in the liturgy by virtue of their identity as women.

A second example of evocative but inadequately explicated symbols is found in Miriam Therese Winter's *Circle of Love,* in which she writes:

> (Set up chairs to form two concentric circles that face each other. The inner circle should face outward and the outer circle should face inward. When it is time for the ritual to begin, invite people to take their places and to enter into silence. The room should be bathed in the warm glow of a whole array of candles. Savor the stillness, and begin . . .)
> The circle of love
> is repeatedly broken
> because of the sin
> of exclusion . . .
> (rearrange the chairs into a single circle, facing in . . . stand in front of the chairs.)
> Lift up your hearts to the One Holy God . . .
> Open yourselves to be touched by Her word.
> Surrender yourselves to Her presence within. . . .[25]

Winter wrote her ritual primarily but not solely for women, unlike the one from *Women-Church.* Neither one is intended as a "primary rite," to use Winter's words, and as her liturgy progresses, a variety of explanations are given for the circle. The organizing principle for selecting these referents and not others is not given, however. This indicates that the people participating in the rites are "insiders"; they know without being told what the symbols mean, or, as suggested earlier, know they are free to assign whatever meaning has private significance for them. Such an understanding of liturgy seems contrary to the corporate and inclusive-missionary nature of a more traditional theology of Christian public worship.

A fourth principle operating in many liberation and radical feminist liturgies is rejection of Victor Turner's concept of liminality.[26] Litanies of remembrance and prophetic challenges from the designated leader of worship serve to remind participants of who they are, not calls to be something else. Women are encouraged to claim their "true selves" rather than submit to oppressive patriarchy. In such feminist liturgies, the congregation does not progress through a time and place set-apart; the experience is not one of transformation, but of affirmation. For example, during the 1987 United Methodist Clergywomen's Consultation, a prayer of confession during worship contained the following:

> I've let myself be redefined—by what it takes to maintain the institution and please the folks—I've lost sight of all the rest . . . I haven't read poetry in ages—not laughed or wept with a friend. . . . [27]

For "words of assurance," participants turned to one another and declared, "I am who I am—doing what I came to do." The rejection of liturgy as liminal experience may be rooted in the determination to affirm as good and worthy what patriarchal clericalism long deemed inferior.

The fifth operating principle in liberation feminist liturgy is that Scripture must be used very selectively in worship or discarded altogether. Women are warned against "indiscriminate reading of Scripture, which often affirms the inferiority and evil nature of women."[28] This cautious or skeptical attitude toward the Bible may come from different sources. First, most obviously, is the hermeneutic of suspicion discussed in the chapter on interpretation. The Bible is seen as an ancient and patriarchal document; many of its texts mitigate against women, affirming their inferiority and legitimizing oppression. "Liberating texts" must be used to address oppressive ones, or the misogynist passages renounced. For example, Christology is a key issue for liberation feminists and rejectionists. A preacher of this orientation may want to react against a hermeneutic that declares women should not preach because Jesus did not choose women among the Twelve. Rather than taking aim at Jesus Christ per se, a woman may use other texts and resources as part of her hermeneutic of suspicion, to correct this misogynist understanding of the person and work of Christ.

A second reason for practicing selectivity in using the Bible is awareness of the biases that operate in any lectionary. For example, in the *Common Lectionary* Year B (published 1983), there were fourteen Sundays in which the story of David from I and II Samuel was read. David's adultery with Bathsheba was included, but the lectionary skipped over the rape of Tamar. The Judges 19 text describing the rape and dismemberment of the Levite's concubine was omitted from the lectionary, as was any mention of Deborah the prophetess and judge (Judges 4) or Miriam's dance and song of praise (Exodus 15:19-21). The lectionary offered a very limited depiction of women, one which turned a blind eye to violence against them and offered few positive role models. Reverse selectivity, manifested in alternative lectionaries, was the solution prescribed by some liberation feminists.

The third reason for limited and selected use of the Bible for preaching and liturgy is a perceived lack of mandate in Scripture itself. The claim is sometimes made that the Bible itself provides no liturgical patterns for Christian worship (I Corinthians 11 and 14 notwithstanding).[29] The variety of preaching styles recorded in the New Testament, as well as the pragmatism manifested by Paul in his sermon at Mars Hill, are taken as a green light for whatever contextualizing a community deems desirable. Within this frame of reference, a feminist may attribute high authority to selected portions of Scripture but have insufficient knowledge about the first-century church to discern when a text is speaking to its liturgical context or her own.

A fourth reason for cropping texts or not using them at all is that there are other loci of authority for preacher and/or congregation. Chief among these is personal experience or intuition, as demonstrated by this advice by one clergywoman:

> Because the amount of repetition and the investment in a phrase is very great, it is important to ask *what effect a particular phrase seems to have upon you.* You ought never to choose a phrase which

is stated in the negative form, such as "lead me out of temptation."
Rather, you should state what you do want; in this case, "God
leads me toward the good."[30]

By this criterion, the Lord's Prayer would not be repeated often by
a worshiping community, because the phrase "lead us not into
temptation" is negative. Though the writer expresses appreciation
for the variety of metaphors for the Deity found in the Bible, and
displays knowledge of biblical and early church tradition,
incorporating these data is contingent on how it feels to an
individual. Guidelines are not given for corporate prayer if it feels
radically different to various participants. Locating a "discon-
nected" authority in oneself is also indicated in the suggestions for
reflection and action in this prayer manual; the reader is advised to
experiment with saying the Jesus Prayer, the Rosary, or other life
mantras without theological reflection on how the church has
historically understood and used each of these.

One issue that has been touched on briefly before is the
ambiguity of some feminist liturgies concerning Christology. The
ambiguity may be a by-product of general alienation from
mainstream worship. A high Christology may be antithetical to the
relationship of mutuality with God presented in some worship
resources, or a reaction against the particularity of the maleness of
the Incarnate Messiah. In any case, the result in many (though not
all) contemporary feminist liturgies is a vague or truncated
Christology. This is in contrast to the Christocentric nature of
classical Christian worship.[31] An example of the diminished
centrality of Christ in feminist liturgy is found in one collection of
lectionary aids for Easter Sunday. Although some prayers
conclude with the traditional "through Jesus Christ our Lord," the
call to worship, invocation, litany, and benediction do not
explicitly acknowledge that Jesus Christ rose from the dead.
Metaphorical language that can be interpreted any number of ways
is substituted, as an excerpt from the invocation demonstrates:

> Today we gather together not merely to applaud your choice but to
> ask for its repetition in us. Deliver us from the self-righteous
> addiction of the crucifiers that we might know that self-giving

161

affection of the Crucified. Grant us the power to proclaim the Easter promise of participation in the conquest of Christ by living out the commitment of Jesus.[32]

The final characteristic of this radical or liberation feminist approach to liturgy is closely related to the one previously discussed: there is a fluid and transitory sense of authority in making liturgical decisions. Feminist liturgy is experimental: not casual, but understood as steps along the way rather than finished products.[33] The intensity with which feminists pursue contextuality means that rituals and words are often understood to be nontransferable to other gatherings or occasions. Only a fraction of the liturgies developed are ever published, and they appear in print with the invitation to use them to stimulate creativity rather than as blueprints. As Arlene Swidler notes in the preface to *Sistercelebrations,* her anthology is not a collection of services from which women just choose something to replay for their own group. They were published in the hope that women's groups would take the time to reassess their personal and communal goals for themselves.[34]

In the same vein, Ruether writes that covenanted communities should work out a basic credal statement that is revised at each recovenanting. For gatherings of groups that are not ongoing communities, credal statements can be developed specifically for an occasion.[35] Though this degree of sensitivity to context may seem laudable on the surface, it points to an underlying relativism that is contrary to the truth claims of the historic Christian faith. One feminist who co-authored a book of lectionary aids advised her readers:

> Alter these prayers *in any way* that will make them more fully your own—by changing the language for addressing deity, by deleting or editing or substituting paragraphs, by localizing the points of reference.[36]

Either the author assumes the reader already knows and uses appropriate criteria for determining what changes should be made in a particular context, or she doesn't acknowledge the legitimacy of any external criteria.

The degrees of flexibility, contextuality, and shared authority valued by feminists are understandable. They manifest themselves as a corrective to clericalism and publishers functioning as a liturgical elite. They enable worship to take the experiences and aspirations of women seriously, and give voice to a portion of the church long exhorted to be silent. At the same time, such liturgy deprives the ship of faith of a palpable anchor, and risks being "tossed to and fro and carried about with every wind of doctrine" (Ephesians 4:14). Though liberated from the strictures of patriarchy, such liturgies are vulnerable to faddism, the oppression of individual idiosyncrasy, and unwitting heresy.

IMPLICATIONS FOR WOMEN AND LITURGY

Feminist and nonfeminist women have demonstrated that their theological/political orientations can find expression using most of the liturgical patterns of western Christianity. The pattern of worship that is not compatible with women's expression of their orientation is the Roman Mass, since women are not allowed to preside. These liturgical structures are used on a weekly basis. They facilitate a balance of prophetic and pastoral concerns; those at worship are familiar with the pattern, so they are more ready to hear "different" content within the structure. The preacher can create a balance between the familiar and the novel. The relationship between sermon and liturgy can be didactic as well as coherent and aesthetically pleasing.

The woman preacher who stays within these patterns runs at least three risks, however. The first is getting into a rut; she may let the structure of the service dictate the content to a degree that, like the preacher with two or three hobbyhorses, the congregation can predict what she'll say next. The second risk is allowing portions of the service to be done by rote, thus losing their evocative power for the congregation. The third genuine risk is regression into patriarchy. A preacher (male or female) who is tired of being attentive to exclusiveness and oppression, or weary of "representing" feminism to the congregation, turns a blind eye to words and acts that have no place in the worship of God.

The feminist principles that can lead to "blurred lines" in worship also have their strengths and liabilities. Although, as most creators of these liturgies acknowledge, they are not designed with Sunday morning worship in mind, some of the material could be adapted for seasonal or occasional use in the local church. Though the flexibility and spontaneity valued in these liturgies is not limited to one theological/political orientation, the principles shaping the liturgies reflect a radical or liberation feminist point of view. A woman considering incorporation of *any* new worship materials should ask herself whether this will be one-time use or become a standard part of worship. The spontaneity encouraged by feminist liturgists almost inevitably evolves into either (a) a fixed structure with rules and logic of its own—hardly the contextual, serendipitous word-act it once was; or (b) something viewed as a temporary aberration, recalled chiefly for the feelings it evoked among those at worship. Neither one serves a feminist agenda.

A liberation feminist may be perceived as rejecting historic confessions of Christian faith (and encounter far greater personal and institutional opposition) if she does not attend to several issues in creating materials and leading people in worship. First, the language and symbols used in feminist liturgy should be interpreted adequately for the congregation to understand and have opportunity to claim them as their own. Second, though contextuality is valued in feminist theology, it should be balanced with "universality" or values and practices shared with other Christian communities, so that liturgy will not be perceived as the idiosyncratic expression of one person or select group. In the same way, preaching and liturgy should communicate that one's identity in the community that meets Sunday morning is based on one's faith commitment—not on sex, race, or insider's knowledge. The immanence of God should not be celebrated at the expense of divine transcendence that is present for other people in other places and times, yet not limited by their perception or ours.

The absence of Scripture, or the appearance of manipulating texts or using an unintelligible hermeneutic, will give Sunday morning the appearance of the preacher using the pulpit as a soapbox for personal opinion in a culture for which the Bible serves a powerful iconic function. Congregations are particularly sensitive to interpretations that shortchange their understanding of the nature and work of Jesus Christ. Shedding new light on old texts is a better pastoral and liturgical strategy than shoving unattractive ones into a dark corner. In a similar way, the woman preacher developing or using new worship resources—feminist or otherwise—should keep in mind the Christocentric nature of Christian worship. She will be wise to contemplate what is being said or left unsaid about the object of people's faith.

Finally, women leading worship should ponder the pedagogical and transformative functions of liturgy. People come to worship expecting something to happen; the element of transformation or deliverance (Turner's "liminality") is a significant, though often unarticulated hope. Declarations such as "I am who I am, doing what I came to do" deprive a congregation of divine promises. The transformative element of liturgy may be expressed in different ways. Prayers, readings, and hymns that announce and prepare for God's interaction with humanity help a congregation to grasp and claim that interaction. Worship materials that untangle traditions used unjustly to bind women or others reflect God's unfolding purpose for creation, and enable the people to respond with thanksgiving and commitment to participate in God's ongoing work of redemption and liberation.

NOTES

INTRODUCTION

1. Conrad Massa, "Preaching As Confluence," inaugural address in *Princeton Seminary Bulletin,* 1979.

CHAPTER 1: THE CALL TO PREACH

1. *The Flyer,* General Commission on the Status and Role of Women in The United Methodist Church, December 1989, p. 3.
2. ATS Survey, David S. Schuller, ed., *Theological Education* (Vandalia, Ohio: The Association of Theological Schools, Spring 1988), p. 40.
3. Carol Norén, "The Self-Image of Women Preachers" (Princeton Theological Seminary, 1983).
4. America Tapia-Ruano, interview with author, Summer 1984.
5. Charles D. Hackett, ed., *Women of the Word: Contemporary Sermons by Women Clergy* (Atlanta: Susan Hunter Publishing, 1985), p. 139.
6. David Albert Farmer and Edwina Hunter, *And Blessed Is She: Sermons by Women* (San Francisco: Harper & Row, 1990), p. 239.
7. Judith Weidman, ed., *Women Ministers* (San Francisco: Harper & Row, 1985), p. 71.
8. Isabel Carter Heyward, *A Priest Forever* (San Francisco: Harper & Row, 1976), p. 3.
9. Elsie Gibson, *When the Minister Is a Woman* (New York: Holt, Rinehart and Winston, 1970), pp. 57 and 58.
10. Nancy Hardesty, *Women Called to Witness* (Nashville: Abingdon Press, 1984), p. 88.
11. Letha Dawson Scanzoni, and Susan Setta, "Women in Evangelical, Holiness, and Pentecostal Traditions," in Rosemary Radford Ruether and Rosemary Skinner Keller, eds., *Women and Religion in America, Volume 3: A Documentary History* (San Francisco: Harper & Row, 1986), p. 226.
12. "Testimony of Mrs. William E. Fisher" in Donald Dayton, ed., *Holiness Tracts Defending the Ministry of Women,* pp. 62-64.
13. William L. Andrews, ed., *Sisters of the Spirit: Three Black Women's Autobiographies of the Nineteenth Century* (Bloomington, Ind.: Indiana University Press, 1986), p. 37.
14. Jean Miller Schmidt, "Grace Sufficient," lecture at Duke University, October 29, 1990.

15. Phoebe Palmer, *Promise of the Father: or, A Neglected Specialty of the Last Days*, in Nancy Hardesty, *Women Called to Witness: Evangelical Feminism in the 19th Century* (Nashville: Abingdon Press, 1984), p. 94.
16. Ibid.
17. Aimee Semple McPherson, *This Is That: Personal Experiences, Sermons and Writings* (Los Angeles: Echo Park Evangelistic Association, Inc., 1923), p. 73.

CHAPTER 2: ROLE MODELS AND THE WOMAN PREACHER

1. Jackson W. Carroll, Barbara Hargrove, and Adair T. Lummis, *Women of the Cloth* (San Francisco: Harper & Row, 1983), p. 224.
2. Harry Hale Jr., Morton King, and Doris Moreland Jones, *Clergywomen: Problems and Satisfactions* (Lima, Ohio: Fairway Press, 1985), p. 72.
3. Rosemary Radford Ruether, *Women-Church: Theology and Practice of Feminist Liturgical Communities* (New York: Harper & Row, 1985), p. 207.
4. Joan Chittister, O.S.B., *Womanstrength: Modern Church, Modern Women* (Kansas City, Mo.: Sheed and Ward, 1990), p. 28.
5. Priscilla Lane Denham, "It's Hard to Sing the Song of Deborah," in *Spinning a Sacred Yarn: Women Speak from the Pulpit* (New York: Pilgrim Press, 1982), p. 63.
6. Miriam Therese Winter, *Woman Prayer, Woman Song: Resources for Ritual* (Oak Park, Ill.: Meyer Stone and Company, Inc., 1987), pp. 115-42.
7. Mary Trum, "Mary of Bethany—A Woman of Faith," sermon excerpt, March 1991.
8. Julian of Norwich, *Revelations of Divine Love* (St. Meinrad, Ind.: Abbey Press, 1961), chap. 59.
9. Ibid., chap. 58.
10. Isabel Carter Heyward, "Learning to See," in Farmer and Hunter, *And Blessed Is She*, p. 171.
11. Interview with "Harrietta," in Norén, "The Self-Image of Women Preachers."
12. Carol M. Norén, survey of women in introductory preaching class, 1991.
13. The Reverend Åsa Jonsson, interview with author, Uppsala, Sweden, August 1990.
14. Martha B. Kriebel, *A Stole Is a Towel: Lessons Learned in the Parish Ministry* (New York: The Pilgrim Press, 1988), p. 18.
15. Carroll, Hargrove, and Lummis, *Women of the Cloth*, p. 230. Of the women surveyed in *Women of the Cloth*, 47 percent were solo pastors of a church, which meant they were responsible for preaching every Sunday and could not take the occasional week off to go hear another woman in the pulpit. Though an even higher percentage of men surveyed (66 percent) were solo pastors, men have not grown up without the opportunity to hear others of their sex preach.
16. A 1970 doctrinal study of twenty-five high level women executives revealed that all had attached very strongly in their early careers to a male boss. Once in the protective custody of this mentor, they subordinated all other relationships to it. See Margaret Henning, "Career Development for Women Executives," Graduate School of Business Administration at Harvard University, 1970, quoted in Gail Sheehy, *Passages: the Predictable Crisis of Adult Life* (New York: E.P. Dutton & Company, 1974), p. 190. But "subordinating all other relationships" is not permissible or healthy for women or men in ordained ministry. Furthermore, a strong attachment between a (usually) younger, single woman and an older, (usually) married man in the church—however honorable—is likely to be misconstrued by outsiders.
17. Ibid.
18. Gail Sheehy noted that professional men had to "shed" their mentors by age forty, or they would forever be in the mentor's shadow. Sheehy, *Passages*, p. 192.

CHAPTER 3: CLAIMING AND EXERCISING AUTHORITY

1. Interview with Harrietta in Norén, "The Self-Image of Women Preachers."
2. Lynn N. Rhodes, *Co-Creating: A Feminist Vision of Ministry* (Philadelphia: Westminster Press, 1987), p. 27.
3. Christine M. Smith, *Weaving the Sermon: Preaching in a Feminist Perspective* (Louisville: Westminster/John Knox Press, 1989), pp. 46 and 47.
4. Martha Long Ice, *Clergy Women and Their Worldviews* (New York: Greenwood Press, Inc., 1987), p. 81.
5. Carroll, Hargrove, and Lummis, *Women of the Cloth*, p. 238. An identical percentage of the 739 men surveyed gave an equally high evaluation of their effectiveness.
6. Interviews with "Hildegarde" and "Carol" in Norén, "The Self-Image of Women Preachers."
7. Mary Rowe Miller, interview with author, March 1991.
8. Rhodes, *Co-Creating*, p. 31.
9. Carroll, Hargrove, and Lummis, *Women of the Cloth*, pp. 238 and 239. In two of these three categories, male clergy reported a higher degree of confidence.
10. Sheehy, *Passages*, pp. 164 and 165.
11. Carroll, Hargrove, and Lummis, *Women of the Cloth*, p. 251. Parenthetically, the fear noted by Sheehy that "no one will marry a woman if she's too successful and independent" may be a realistic one for clergywomen. Jackson W. Carroll's survey, published in 1983, revealed that 45 percent of women clergy were unmarried, and 32 percent of them had never been married. Only 6 percent of male clergy were unmarried, and 4 percent never married. A perusal of seminary student directories also suggests that male seminarians are far more likely to be married than female students. These surveys do not indicate whether one is single by choice.
12. Carol Gilligan, *In a Different Voice: Psychological Theory and Women's Development* (Cambridge, Mass.: Harvard University Press, 1982), p. 11.
13. Ice, *Clergy Women and Their Worldviews*, p. 88.
14. Ibid., p. 95.
15. World Council of Churches Studies, no. 4, *The Deaconess. A Service of Women in the World of Today* (Geneva, 1966), p. 12.
16. Gibson, *When the Minister Is a Woman*, p. 25.
17. Judith Ruhe Diehl, *A Woman's Place* (Philadelphia: Fortress Press, 1985), p. 15.

CHAPTER 4: SELF-DISCLOSURE IN WOMEN'S PREACHING

1. Mechthild Babb, "Which Way to God?" sermon on Mark 8:31-39, February, 1991.
2. This is not to say that an illustration must never be purely autobiographical. The first-person story can be an effective device for engaging a congregation and setting people at ease, particularly with a new preacher. In "representative I" statements, however, listeners must be able to say, "Yes, that's me," giving assent to the reflection she presents to them.
3. Diana Trebbi, "My Prayer 'Grows Up' as I Grow Older," in *Spinning a Sacred Yarn*, pp. 212-15.
4. Rebecca Dolch, "Offer Them Christ: The Blood of Christ," sermon excerpt, November, 1987.
5. Christine Smith, "Redemptive Songs," in Farmer and Hunter, *And Blessed Is She*, p. 223.
6. Nancy Barnard Starr, "Jesus Cleanses the Temple," sermon on John 2:13-22, February, 1991.

7. LaTaunya M. Bynum, "The Church: The Family of God," sermon on II Corinthians 6:14–7:1, in Farmer and Hunter, *And Blessed Is She*, p. 119.
8. Rita Nakashima Brock, "Courage/Commitment," sermon on Ruth 1:1-19 and Matthew 22:15-22, in Farmer and Hunter, *And Blessed Is She*, pp. 109-11.
9. Rebecca Dolch, "Offer Them Christ: The Blood of Christ," sermon excerpt, November, 1987.
10. Donna Jones, "Signs of the Times," sermon on Luke 21:25-36, 1989.
11. Camille S. Littleton, sermon on Amos 7:7-15 in Hackett, *Women of the Word*, p. 70.
12. Eloise Hally, sermon on John 4:5-26 in Hackett, *Women of the Word*, p. 39.
13. Leontine T. C. Kelly, "No Bulls, No Lambs, No Goats," in Farmer and Hunter, *And Blessed Is She*, p. 179.
14. Tallulah Fisher-Williams, "Shake and Bake," sermon on Acts 28:1-6, DeKalb, Ill., June, 1989.
15. Marianne LaFrance, "Gender Gestures: Sex, Sex-Role, and Nonverbal Communication," in Clara Mayo and Nancy M. Henley, eds., *Gender and Nonverbal Behavior* (New York: Springer-Verlag, 1981), pp. 130 and 132.
16. Maxine Walaskay, "Gender and Preaching," in *The Christian Ministry*, January 1982, p. 9.
17. W. Jardine Grisbrooke, "Vestments," in Cheslyn Jones, Geoffrey Wainwright, and Edward Yarnold, *The Study of Liturgy* (New York: Oxford University Press, 1978), p. 488.
18. Alison Lurie, *The Language of Clothes* (New York: Vintage Books, 1983), pp. 214-15.
19. Thomas Troeger, "We Had to Sacrifice the Woman," *The Christian Century*, February 4-11, 1981, p. 108.
20. Ruether, *Women-Church*, p. 159.
21. Interview with "Lucy" in Norén, "The Self-Image of Women Preachers."
22. Jeanette Jones Haviland and Carol Zander Malatests, "The Development of Sex Differences in Nonverbal Signals: Fallacies, Facts, and Fantasies," in Clara Mayo and Nancy Henley, *Gender and Nonverbal Behavior*, (New York: Springer-Verlag, Inc., 1981), pp. 187-88.
23. Rita Mae Brown, "The Good Fairy," *Quest*, 1974, I, pp. 61 and 62.
24. Evie Tornquist-Karlsson, "Four Feet Eleven," on *Mirror*, Word Records, 1977.
25. The higher intonation, occasionally used with "tag" questions, is discussed in the chapter on theology in metaphor and grammar.
26. Smith, *Weaving the Sermon*, p. 133.
27. Brown, "The Good Fairy," pp. 61 and 62.
28. Troeger, "We Had to Sacrifice the Woman," p. 124.
29. The cultural limitations of this description of body language must be acknowledged. Gender-related differences in gesture seem to occur around the globe, but a different "set" of gestures may be considered masculine or feminine in various cultures.

CHAPTER 5: WOMEN PREACHERS AND BIBLICAL INTERPRETATION

1. Farmer and Hunter, *And Blessed Is She*, pp. 89-90.
2. Ibid., pp. 94 and 95.
3. Justo L. Gonzalez, and Catherine G. Gonzalez, *Liberation Preaching: The Pulpit and the Oppressed* (Nashville: Abingdon Press, 1980), p. 99.
4. Smith, *Weaving the Sermon*, p. 9.
5. Jacquelyn Grant, *White Women's Christ and Black Women's Jesus: Feminist Christology and Womanist Response* (Atlanta: Scholars Press, 1989), pp. 4 and 5.

6. Elisabeth Schüssler Fiorenza, *Bread Not Stone: The Challenge of Feminist Biblical Interpretation* (Boston: Beacon Press, 1984), pp. x and xi.
7. Phyllis Trible, "The Pilgrim Bible on a Feminist Journey," *Daughters of Sarah* 15.3 (May/June 1989) :5-7.
8. Sehested in Farmer and Hunter, *And Blessed Is She*, pp. 212-14.
9. Juan Luis Segundo, *The Liberation of Theology* (Maryknoll, N.Y.: Orbis Books, 1976), p. 9.
10. Phyllis Trible, *God and the Rhetoric of Sexuality* (Philadelphia: Fortress Press, 1978), p. 167.
11. Carole Carlson in *Spinning a Sacred Yarn*, pp. 10-13.
12. Schüssler Fiorenza, *Bread Not Stone*, p. 21.
13. Gonzalez, *Liberation Preaching*, p. 69.
14. Constance George in Ella Pearson Mitchell, ed., *Those Preaching Women: More Sermons by Black Women Preachers*, vol. 2 (Valley Forge, Pa.: Judson Press, n.d.), pp. 70-71.
15. Gonzalez, *Liberation Preaching*, p 83.
16. In cataloging sermon texts from *Spinning a Sacred Yarn, And Blessed Is She, Those Preaching Women* and *Women of the Word*, I discovered there were approximately as many sermons on narrative texts as on purely didactic and prophetic texts combined. The more frequent use of New Testament texts than Old may reflect the current tendency to preach the Gospel lesson as often as possible.
17. Yolande Herron-Palmore in Mitchell, *Those Preaching Women*, pp. 41-43.
18. Rosemary Radford Ruether, "Woman as Oppressed; Woman as Liberated in the Scriptures," in *Spinning a Sacred Yarn*, p. 186.
19. Gonzalez, *Liberation Preaching*, p. 78.
20. Karolyn Edwards, "The Text Considered and Spoken," sermon excerpt, April 1988.
21. Carol Norén, "Ministry and Money-changing," sermon excerpt, March 1988.
22. Gonzalez, *Liberation Preaching*, p. 24.
23. Merlene Firebaugh, "The Happy Prince," sermon excerpt, 1988.
24. Barbara Brown Taylor, "Pentecost X" in Hackett, *Women of the Word*, pp. 127-28.
25. This is not to suggest *only* younger preachers employ this method; I have occasionally heard it from older women as well as men. The vocabulary used in retelling the text, along with the tendency to re-enact it in a more familiar context, makes me wonder if the preacher is (a) using it as one means of "getting into the text" herself or (b) trying to cultivate rapport with the congregation by placing herself and/or them in the story.
26. Jenny Copeland, sermon on Luke 17:11-19, Durham, North Carolina, 1987.
27. Shelly Abbey Fogleman, "Dry Bones," sermon on Ezekiel 37, 1988.
28. JoAnn Flora, "It Takes Faith to Walk on Water," sermon excerpt, 1988.
29. Shelly Abbey Fogleman, "One Thing Is Needful," sermon excerpt, November 1988.
30. Margaret Crockett-Cannon, "What Do You Want Me to Do for You?" in *Spinning a Sacred Yarn*, p. 31.
31. JoAnn Flora, sermon excerpt, 1988.
32. E. Claiborne Jones, Pentecost XIV sermon in Hackett, *Women of the Word*, pp. 56-59.
33. Gilligan, *In a Different Voice*, p. 11.
34. Nancy Chodorow, *The Reproduction of Mothering: The Psychoanalysis and the Sociology of Gender* (Berkeley, Calif.: University of California Press, 1976), p. 93.
35. Mary Field Belenky, Blythe McVicker Clinchy, Nancy Rule Goldberger, and Jill Mattuck Tarule, *Women's Ways of Knowing: The Development of Self, Voice and Mind* (New York: Basic Books, 1987), pp. 60 and 54.
36. Kim Mammedaty, "Remember the Sabbath Day," in Farmer and Hunter, *And Blessed Is She*, pp. 199-200.
37. Peggy Way, "You Are Not My God, Jehovah," in *Spinning a Sacred Yarn*, p. 219.

38. Rosemary Radford Ruether, sermon on Acts 1:1-11, Ascension Sunday, 1987.

CHAPTER 6: THEOLOGY IN METAPHOR AND GRAMMAR

1. Elizabeth Achtemeier, "What's Left Behind?" in Farmer and Hunter, *And Blessed Is She,* p. 99.
2. Paige Chargois, "Unshackled!" in Mitchell, *Those Preaching Women,* pp. 66 and 67.
3. Ian Ramsey, *Religious Language* (London: SCM Press, 1957), pp. 183-85.
4. Virginia Mollenkott, *Godding: Human Responsibility and the Bible* (New York: Crossroad, 1987), pp. 52 and 53.
5. Young Ran Woo, "The Expression of the Language of Inequality of Woman and Man: Perspective of a Korean Woman," *Journal of Women and Religion,* 2.1 (Spring 1982) :23.
6. Russell Letty, "The Impossible Possibility," in Helen Grey Crotwell, *Women and the Word—Sermons* (Philadelphia: Fortress Press, 1978), p. 87.
7. Mozella Mitchell, "Provi-dence," in Mitchell, *Those Preaching Women,* p. 49.
8. Rosemary Radford Ruether, "You Shall Call No Man Father," in Crotwell, *Women and the Word,* pp. 92-99.
9. Ruether, *Women-Church,* p. 145.
10. Isabel Carter Heyward, "Learning to See," in Farmer and Hunter, *And Blessed Is She,* p. 171.
11. Carolyn Stahl Bohler, *Prayer on Wings: A Search for Authentic Prayer* (San Diego, California: Luramedia Press, 1990), p. 68.
12. Division of Education and Ministry, National Council of the Churches of Christ in the U.S.A. *An Inclusive Language Lectionary: Readings for Year B,* Revised Edition. Published for the Cooperative Publication Association by John Knox Press, Atlanta, The Pilgrim Press, New York, The Westminster Press, Philadelphia, 1987, p. 6.
13. Nancy Hardesty, *Inclusive Language in the Church* (Atlanta: John Knox Press, 1987), p. 14.
14. Nancy Hardesty, "Just As I Am," in Crotwell, *Women and the Word,* pp. 8 and 9.
15. Gail Ramshaw, "Lutheran Liturgical Prayer and God as Mother," in *Worship 52,* 1978, p. 518.
16. Gail Ramshaw, *Worship: Searching for Language* (Washington, D.C.: The Pastoral Press, 1988), p. 182.
17. Ibid., p. 206.
18. Paul Minear, *Images of the Church in the New Testament* (Philadelphia: Westminster Press, 1960), pp. 23-24, quoted in Susan Thistlethwaite, *Metaphors for the Contemporary Church* (New York: The Pilgrim Press, 1983), p. 11.
19. Smith, *Weaving the Sermon,* p. 30.
20. Sallie McFague, "The World as God's Body," *Christian Century,* July 20-27, 1988.
21. Sallie McFague, *Metaphorical Theology: Models of God in Religious Language* (Philadelphia: Fortress Press, 1982), p. 193.
22. Thistlethwaite, *Metaphors for the Contemporary Church,* p. 15.
23. Barbara King, "Do I Need a Flood?" in Mitchell, *Those Preaching Women,* pp. 55-61.
24. Patsy Sears, "The Dance of Discipleship," sermon on Mark 8:31-37, 1988.
25. An exception to this, of course, is communication on specialized subjects, such as sports. In this type of interaction, communication relies on already shared meanings and vocabulary.
26. Smith, *Weaving the Sermon,* p. 22.
27. Ibid., p. 47.
28. Christine Smith, "The Redemptive Songs We Sing," in Farmer and Hunter, *And Blessed Is She,* p. 227.

29. Ibid., p. 224.
30. Lesley Stahl, in Joan Barthel, "Why There Are Still No Female Dan Rathers," *TV Guide*, August 6-12, 1983, p. 5.
31. Catherine Ziel, "Women in the Pulpit: Some Sociolinguistic Questions," Princeton Theological Seminary, April 1986, p. 4, quoting Diana W. Warshay, "Sex Difference in Language Style," Constantina Safilios-Rothschild, ed., *Toward a Sociology of Women* (Lexington, Massachusetts: Xerox College Publishing, 1972), p. 82.
32. Diana Swancutt, survey of women in introductory preaching class, March 1991.
33. Babb, "Which Way to God?" sermon excerpt, February 1991.
34. Carrie Yearick, sermon on Matthew 13:24-30, 1988.
35. Camille Littleton, sermon on John 9:1-38 in Hackett, *Women of the Word*, p. 68.
36. Flora, "It Takes Faith to Walk on Water," sermon excerpt, August 1988.
37. Diana Swancutt, sermon on John 3:17-24, 1991.
38. Barbara Bate, *Communication and the Sexes* (New York: Harper & Row, 1988), p. 237.

CHAPTER 7: WOMEN PREACHERS AND LITURGY

1. Barbara Brown Zikmund, "Women as Preachers: Adding New Dimensions to Worship," *Journal of Women and Religion*, vol. 3, no. 2, 1989, p. 15.
2. C. Virginia Finn, "A Mass of Freedom for Women," in Arlene Swidler, ed., *Sistercelebrations: Nine Worship Experiences* (Philadelphia: Fortress Press, 1974), pp. 31-34.
3. Finn in Swidler, *Sistercelebrations*, p. 32.
4. Geoffrey Wainwright, "The Understanding of Liturgy in the Light of Its History," Jones, Wainwright, and Yarnold, eds., *The Study of Liturgy*, pp. 503-6.
5. Rebecca Dolch, "The Blood of Christ," sermon excerpt, October 1988.
6. Sharon Brown Christopher, and Leontine T. C. Kelly, "Closing Worship Celebration," National Clergywomen's Consultation, The United Methodist Church, Feburary 1983.
7. Janet Morley, *All Desires Known* (London: Movement for the Ordination of Women, 1988), p. 10.
8. Ibid., p. 14.
9. Shelly Abbey Fogleman, "One Thing Is Needful," sermon excerpt, November 1988.
10. Aimee Semple McPherson, "A Typical Weekend in Angelus Temple," *This Is That*, pp. 540-42.
11. Miriam Therese Winter, *Woman Prayer Woman Song: Resources for Ritual* (Oak Park, Ill.: Meyer Stone and Company, 1987), p. 206.
12. Isabel Carter Heyward, "Blessing the Bread," in Iben Gjerding and Katherine Kinnamon, eds., *No Longer Strangers: A Resource for Women and Worship* (Geneva: WCC Publications, 1984), p. 22.
13. Geoffrey Wainwright, "Theology of Worship," in J. G. Davies, *New Westminster Dictionary of Liturgy and Worship* (Philadelphia: Westminster Press, 1986), p. 505.
14. Sharon Zimmerman Rader, "Generations of Women Shaping Church," in *Wellsprings: A Journal of United Methodist Clergywomen*, vol. 3, no. 2 (Nashville: Division of Ordained Ministry, The United Methodist Church, 1990).
15. Janet R. Walton, "The Challenge of Feminist Liturgy," in *Liturgy: Journal of the Liturgical Conference*, vol. 6, no. 1 (The Church and Culture, 1986), pp. 55, 56.
16. Marjorie Procter-Smith, *In Her Own Rite: Constructing Feminist Liturgical Tradition* (Nashville: Abingdon Press, 1990), p. 6.
17. Ibid., p. 133.
18. Ruether, *Women-Church*, p. 129.
19. Bohler, *Prayer on Wings*, p. 8.

20. Mildred E. Nero Drinkard, *Wellsprings: A Journal of United Methodist Clergywomen*, vol. 3, no. 2 (Nashville: Division of Ordained Ministry, The United Methodist Church, 1990), p. 30.
21. Alan Richardson, "Creeds," in *New Westminster Dictionary of Liturgy and Worship* (Philadelphia: Westminster Press, 1986), p. 199.
22. Procter-Smith, *In Her Own Rite*, p. 17.
23. Ibid., p. 23.
24. Ruether, *Women-Church*, p. 221.
25. Winter, *Woman Prayer Woman Song*, pp. 185-88.
26. Victor Turner, "Passages, Margins, and Poverty: Religious Symbols of Communitas," in *Worship*, vol. 46, nos. 7 and 8. Turner described liminal intervals in worship as ritual periods when social structures operating in a culture are suspended. During an encounter with the divine, the identity of the worshiper is expunged, reinterpreted, or replaced by a new identity. As a result of this religious "rite of passage" the self-understandings of the individual and the community are transformed.
27. "Litany of Confession," Consultation Worship Music and Arts Committee, 1987 Clergywomen's Consultation Resource Book, pp. 19-20, quoted in *Wellsprings*, vol. I, no. 1, p. 50.
28. Walton, "The Challenge of Feminist Liturgy," p. 58.
29. Procter-Smith, *In Her Own Rite*, p. 14.
30. Bohler, *Prayer on Wings*, p. 109.
31. See Geoffrey Wainwright, *Doxology: The Praise of God in Worship, Doctrine, and Life* (New York: Oxford University Press, 1980), chap. 2. By Christocentric, I mean worship in which the risen Christ is confessed as Lord at baptism (Acts 16:30-33), invoked as Lord in the Christian assembly (Philippians 2:5-11), worshiped as mediator (I Timothy 2:5, 6; Ephesians 2:18; Hebrews 10:19-22), and is the pattern for Christian worship, particularly the sacraments (Matthew 28:19; I Corinthians 12:12-31).
32. Everett Tilson and Phyllis Cole, *Litanies and Other Prayers for the Common Lectionary* (Nashville: Abingdon Press, 1990), p. 82.
33. Procter-Smith, *In Her Own Rite*, p. 10.
34. Swidler, *Sistercelebrations*, p. vi.
35. Ruether, *Women-Church*, p. 143.
36. Tilson and Cole, *Litanies and Other Prayers for the Common Lectionary*, p. 13.

SUGGESTED READING

Andrews, William L., ed. *Sisters of the Spirit: Three Black Women's Autobiographies of the Nineteenth Century.* Bloomington, Ind.: Indiana University Press, 1986.

Belenky, Mary Field, Blythe McVicker Clinchy, Nancy Rule Goldberger, Jill Mattuck Tarule. *Women's Ways of Knowing: The Development of Self, Voice and Mind.* New York: Basic Books, 1986.

Carroll, Jackson W., Barbara Hargrove, Adair T. Lummis. *Women of the Cloth.* San Francisco: Harper & Row, 1983.

Chittister, Joan, O.S.B. *Womanstrength: Modern Church, Modern Women.* Kansas City, Mo.: Sheed and Ward, 1990.

Grant, Jacquelyn. *White Women's Christ and Black Women's Jesus: Feminist Christology and Womanist Response.* Atlanta: Scholars Press, 1989.

Hardesty, Nancy. *Women Called to Witness.* Nashville: Abingdon Press, 1984.

Hopko, Anthony, ed. *Women and the Priesthood.* New York: St. Vladimir's Seminary Press, 1983.

Ice, Martha Long. *Clergy Women and Their Worldviews.* New York: Praeger Publishers (Greenwood Press, Inc.), 1987.

Ruether, Rosemary Radford. *Women-Church: Theology and Practice.* New York: Harper & Row, 1985.

Schuller, David S., ed. ATS Survey. *Theological Education.* Vandalia, Ohio: The Association of Theological Schools, Fall 1988.